EDUCATORS

healing

racism

edited by

NANCY L. QUISENBERRY
and
D. JOHN MCINTYRE

WITHDRAWN
WRIGHT STATE UNIVERSITY LIBRARIES

A JOINT PUBLICATION OF THE

Association of Teacher Educators
1900 Association Dr., Ste. ATE, Reston, VA 20191
703-620-3110

AND

Association for Childhood Education International
17904 Georgia Ave., Ste. 215, Olney, MD 20832
800-423-3563 • www.udel.edu/bateman/acei

acknowledgments

A number of people have contributed to the production of this publication and the editors gratefully acknowledge their role in the process. Discussions by members of the ATE Commission on Racism from a Healing Perspective led to the outline for the publication. The following persons attended the commission meetings and contributed to the discussion and planning: Jan Towslee, Sylvia P. Swinton, Shelley Clemson, James B. Boyer, Phyllis Y. Hammonds, Norvella Carter, Pat Larke, Anne Gayles-Felton, Robert Hilliard, Gwen Trotter, Larry Vold, Prentice Baptiste, Emily Patterson Harris, John Hendricks, Beverly Klug, G. Pritchy Smith, Fr. Clarence Williams, Paul Woods, Porter L. Troutman, Jr., Gwendolyn Webb-Johnson, and Fredda D. Carroll. Diogenes Lima, Graduate Assistant from SIUC, taped the commission proceedings.

As the work progressed, two members volunteered to review chapters in progress. The editors are appreciative of the reviews completed by Janet Towslee and Hans Olson.

The Illinois Association of Teacher Educators awarded a Minigrant to the Editors, which supported some of the research and dissemination of the case studies and activities cited in the publication. Their support and recognition of the importance of this work were especially appreciated.

Finally, the individuals who were most helpful in the final production of the manuscript were Connie Foran, the Dean's secretary in the College of Education at SIUC, and Michelle Swain and Darren James, Graduate Assistants to the Editor who spent numerous hours scanning draft copies, proofing, checking copy, contacting authors, and providing the editors with help when needed. To these three, we give our thanks.

—N.L.O. & D.J.M.

dedication

To Rose Duhon-Sells

Mother, Wife, Sister, Daughter, Colleague

This book is dedicated to Dr. Rose Duhon-Sells, Past President of the Association of Teacher Educators and now Professor at McNeese State University, Lake Charles, Louisiana. Rose has addressed myriad problems during her formative and professional years. Her approach always has been distinctive and unique. The following quote* best describes Rose's approach: "When you see an arrow that is not going to miss you, throw out your chest and meet it head on." In this spirit, Rose willfully, carefully, and sensitively called together a group of individuals to discuss the concept of "saving our children." One of her concerns was racism, which can attack and destroy people of all ages, genders, and nationalities. Rose also wanted to discuss the need to view racism from a healing perspective. Hence, she established, under the auspices of the Association of Teacher Educators, a Commission on Racism From a Healing Perspective. She crafted the ground rules and expectations for this commission, with the specific goals of studying racism from a healing perspective and then writing a book that would assist educators in "meeting the arrow, head on."

Rose has inspired large numbers of educators from diverse perspectives to unite in studying the issue of racism. She created and nurtured the group with a vision. You will encounter this vision as you struggle with many of the concepts in this book. Rose always has been part of the solution in personal and professional areas. This book is dedicated to her for assisting us in studying and coming to understand different perspectives on racism. We are, and must be, prepared to meet the challenges offered by racism. Rose Duhon-Sells has added strength, courage, and vision to our preparation.

Gwendolyn Trotter,
Central Michigan University

*See *My Soul Looks Back, 'Less I Forget: A Collection of Quotations by People of Color* (Harper Perennial, 1991).

foreword

This publication is the outcome of an idea and a mission established by Rose Duhon-Sells on the eve of assuming the Presidency of the Association of Teacher Educators (ATE). One morning, in Colorado, while we were both serving on an NCATE Board of Examiners team, Rose and I sat at breakfast together. While we ate, Rose described a commission she wanted to appoint during her year as President of ATE. She had a passion for helping teacher educators and those who teach and work with children to begin the process of healing racism in the United States. I was intrigued by her ideas and encouraged her to pursue this dream.

The next morning, Rose asked me to chair the Commission, joining her in this quest to prepare materials and suggestions for teachers and teacher educators who truly want to see racism overcome in our society. We both agreed that this would be taking a big step beyond teaching about cultural diversity and multicultural education. The "R" word was not (and still is not) widely used in education circles. Our discussions turned to the makeup of the Commission and the goals we could set for it.

One might ask why a White woman would even consider this task. My history of concern for the differences between the races predates my many years as a teacher and teacher educator. I was privileged to be raised by a mother who, early in my life, taught me the value of loving and recognizing the good in all people. As a little girl barely past toddler stage, I can remember going to visit an "aunt" and "uncle" who were African American. I was taught that these two wonderful people were like family. My father had become good friends with the "uncle" through an organization he belonged to in our town, and we often went to visit them. I also grew up knowing that another African American family in my home town was close to my mother's family, at a time when people of different races in a small southern Indiana town were not always friendly or close. And I grew up knowing the history of our two families—a history that involved my grandmother saving the life of the mother of the African American family from a fire, and the closeness that resulted from being neighbors and sharing such a traumatic experience. I believe that being reared with this attitude toward others has led me to look beyond color in my relationships with people. In turn, this has led to my deep interest in dealing with cultural diversity in education and the desire to prepare others for multicultural settings.

To accept the challenge of chairing the Commission meant I would have to venture well beyond teaching about cultural diversity. Racism is a serious problem in the United States. Only in the past few years have the country's leaders begun to address and discuss it more openly. Many of my generation believe that much more was accomplished in the '60s toward eliminating prejudice than really is evident when we look deeper. Yes, we took stands against segregation in the late '50s and '60s and integration followed, but the feelings of prejudice and hurt remained buried deep in our people's souls.

Discussions among members of the Commission revealed the deep hurt of persons who have suffered from racist slurs and who continue to see this happen to their families and to their students. The naiveté of White educators' beliefs about what has been accomplished to heal society was revealed over and over again. The beauty of the discussions lay in the commissioners' willingness to share experiences and to talk about problems and situations in an open and frank atmosphere. We all grew from this experience.

As the Commission approached its second year, we determined that we needed to share our information and discussions with other teachers and teacher educators. The idea for this publication took shape, and the authors volunteered to work on those sections that were of greatest interest to them. At about this same time, President Clinton began talking about addressing problems of racism in the United States. Almost simultaneously with the development of this publication, town meetings on racism began to spring up around the country, giving credence to our belief that this was the time to address the problem, and try to heal the hurt of those persons who have long suffered from the effects of racism.

It is our dream that the experiences and ideas put forth in this publication will help bring about racial healing in our society. Who better to do this than our teachers and teacher educators?

Nancy L. Quisenberry
Southern Illinois University

introduction

Healing Racism Through Teachers and Teacher Education Programs

In his keynote address at the 1996 Association of Teacher Educators' Conference in St. Louis, G. Pritchy Smith stated that racism cuts deeply into the fabric of American society, and he challenged teachers and teacher educators to have the moral courage to help re-create America as an anti-racist and a more fair, just, and democratic society. In many respects, this text reinforces Pritchy's challenge by having the courage to address the topic of racism from the teacher's perspective, and by proposing strategies for combating this position through teacher education programs and in the classroom. In addition, this text differs from traditional education books that merely address multicultural education and strategies for teaching about other cultures. Instead, the authors deal directly with the problem of racism—a controversial, explosive topic.

Nieto (1996) asserts that the legacy of education history in the United States is fraught with discrimination and racism, and that discrimination in schools is not a thing of the past. It is true, as Nieto asserts, that some of this discrimination is unintentional—for example, a teacher, administrator, or counselor who is not attuned to diversity may make a remark or gesture that is degrading to a child. In spite of their best intentions, teachers and teacher educators often unwittingly perpetuate racist perceptions. Thus, classroom educators should be aware of their attitudes and behaviors and how they might affect a culturally diverse student population.

> **Classroom educators should be aware of their attitudes and behaviors and how they might affect a culturally diverse student population.**

Discussions of racism often provoke anger, guilt, and blame (Tatum, 1992). Although the intention of this text is not to assign blame, the authors hope that it does provoke some anger and some guilt. Mostly, we hope that it engenders a dialogue among education professionals as to how the healing of racism can begin through teacher education programs and, as a result, in classrooms. Rose Duhon-Sells, with Gwendolyn Duhon-Haynes, Alice Duhon-Ross, and Halloway C. Sells, sets the tone for the book by describing studies that recount the pervasiveness of racism in society and in schools. She also provides educators with a list of suggestions and strategies for understanding their own innate biases and for addressing racism and reducing its impact on students. H. Prentice Baptiste, James B. Boyer, Socorro Herrera, and Kevin Murry continue this focus by examining the social, political, and psychological perspectives of racism. They help readers understand how racism has torn at the fabric of society. Although the purpose of this first section is to examine racism's pervasively negative impact, the utility of this book for teachers and teacher educators is reduced if the focus is limited to this pervasiveness. Rather, its utility relies upon the notion proposed by Rose—that although the effects and implications of racism are expansive, they are not irreversible.

Reyes (1991) states that teachers' instructional strategies often can reduce learning opportunities for students from diverse cultures. Section Two examines the healing of racism from instructional perspectives. This section uses case studies as examples of how racism can invade our classrooms, both overtly and covertly. The cases provide powerful examples of critical incidents in children's classroom experiences that adversely affect them for years, and they also provide voices for these disenfranchised students (Nieto, 1996). For example, the chapters by Patricia Larke, Gwendolyn Webb-Johnson, Ronald Rochon, and Mary Anderson, and by Norvella P. Carter, Anne Gayles-Felton, Robert Hilliard, and Larry A. Vold provide poignant case studies of how teachers' statements, or even their classroom activities and strategies, can be unintentionally racist. In Chapter VI, Phyllis Y. Hammonds, Carol Felder, and Fredda D. Carroll also use the case study approach to emphasize not only how racism exists in our schools and teacher education programs, but also, more important, how racism can be addressed in a positive, healing approach through the instructional context. The notion of healing is further explored by Hammonds and Cathy Gutierrez-Gomez as they explore the role of families in the healing process. Finally, the section concludes with a timely example of "what works," in the chapter by Porter Lee Troutman, Richard Powell, Elaine Jarchow, Linda Fussell, and Donna Imatt. The authors describe the efforts of the faculty, administrators, and students at Brown Barge Middle School to create a context that has completely restructured instructional content, the relationships among students, the relationships between teachers and students, and the overall outcomes for learning. This chapter provides a road map for other educators interested in developing an educational context that not only promotes high academic standards, but also fosters the highest levels of multicultural understanding by infusing multiple perspectives throughout all aspects of the curriculum. The Brown Barge Middle School example further emphasizes how certain scenarios can allow the healing process to begin.

No text can be complete without a section on technology and its impact on the subject at hand—in this case, racism. P. Rudy Mattai, Robert L. Perry, and Walter S. Polka address technology and its potential for equalizing opportunities for all students. Access to information and knowledge is power. Without it, people lack the tools—the information and knowledge—to take advantage of opportunities and progress through society. Accordingly, the authors of this chapter discuss the implications for students and communities that do not have technological resources at their fingertips—whether it be in their homes or in their schools.

The text concludes, fittingly, with a challenge from G. Pritchy Smith. Pritchy describes an emotional incident in his life that made him confront his own internalized and unknown racism, and that affected his personal and professional life. In many respects, we all have had such an incident in our lives (maybe not as dramatic as Pritchy's), one that has forced us to re-examine our own belief systems. How we reacted to that personal confrontation may have affected our life's path. In closing, Pritchy again asks, "Who will have the moral courage to heal racism?" He answers that it must be the teachers and teacher educators—those who teach the next generation of teachers and their future students in which line to stand!

D. John McIntyre
Southern Illinois University

Although the intention of this text is not to assign blame, the authors hope that it does provoke some anger and some guilt.

References

Nieto, S. (1996). *Affirming diversity: The sociopolitical context of multicultural education.* White Plains, NY: Longman.

Reyes, D. (1991). Using effective instructional strategies in the multicultural classroom. In J.Q. Adams, J. Niss, & C. Suarez (Eds.), *Multicultural education: Strategies for implementation in colleges and universities* (pp. 17-21). Macomb, IL: Western Illinois University.

Smith, G. P. (1996, February). *Who shall have the moral courage to heal racism in America?* Keynote address presented at the Association of Teacher Educators Conference, St. Louis, MO.

Tatum, B. (1992). Talking about race, learning about racism: The application of racial identity development theory in the classroom. *Harvard Educational Review, 62*(1), 1-24.

Section 1

historical perspectives

chapter 1

Racism in Education

Gwendolyn Duhon-Haynes, *McNeese State University*
Rose Duhon-Sells, *McNeese State University*
Alice Duhon-Ross, *Albany State University*
Halloway C. Sells, *The Union Institute*

Racism in the education system has been long-standing in American history and in other countries where racial differences exist. Oppressive education practices are not only devastating to minority students, but also harmful to students of the majority race. This chapter will begin with a definition of racism and various manifestations of racism. Next, the authors will review early historical documentation on how racism affected the education of both White and Black children, and look at the implications of racism for the current American education system. The authors also will examine strategies for addressing and combating racism in various education settings. Finally, this chapter will examine and outline the various responsibilities of educators, administrators, and school systems in the effort to reduce the impact of racism.

Today's world is extremely diverse, yet the existing social climate in the United States does not readily accept diversity as a reality. Instead, people of color feel pressured to conform, and experience the role confusion, exclusion, isolation, and ethnic and class tensions that frequently lead to violence (Boyer & Baptiste, 1996). Despite increasing diversity, policymakers are moving further and further into a state of denial by not addressing the need for a new paradigm aimed at trying to solve the country's serious social problems. The vast majority of children of color are not being taught in a way that prepares them to participate in the larger society. Some politicians point to this situation to create an atmosphere of fear about the future, rather than focusing on the positive qualities and contributions of each culture.

Education policymakers are capable of helping to heal racism in the schools by implementing new paradigm shifts. Specifically, they can:

- Acknowledge the generations-long struggle of African Americans, the adverse effects of which continue to influence opportunities and lives
- Restructure the content of the curriculum to meet the unique needs of all students, and acknowledge racist policies that block the success of students of color, such as the practices of placing students who misbehave in special education programs and then labeling them as having learning disabilities
- Design faculty development workshops focused on the subtle elements of racism that affect the daily teaching and learning process.

Dube (1985) believes that the concept of racism derives from the myth that mankind is divided into racial subspecies. He defines racism as a psychological phenomenon rooted in the belief that a causal relationship exists between certain inherited physical traits and certain aspects of personality and intellect. This definition includes the notion that some "races" are inherently superior to others, even to the point of superior virtue. Ultimately, those who adhere to this notion believe that superiority is a biologically inherited trait common only to the "virtuous" races.

Dube uses this definition to identify three types of racism: covert, overt, and reactive. Overt racism is open and up-front, while covert racism is very subtle and therefore not easily identified. Reactive racism is sometimes exhibited in the exclusionary tactics of people who themselves have been, or may still be, victims of racism.

McCarthy (1988) discussed the concept of racial ideology, which manifests itself unevenly in educational structures and in the formal and informal practices of school life. Curricula and programs that seek to address racism in school must take into account, for example, the discriminatory effects of what Kevin Brown (1985) calls "White non-racism." "Non-racism" refers to the covert use of racial evaluation that is apparently neutral, but that actually uses coded rhetoric or criteria to discuss minorities. Terms and phrases such as "over-crowding," "welfare mothers," "the lack of experience," or "strain on current resources" are samples of such coded rhetoric.

Racist ideology often is interwoven into various curricula in the schools. Chalmers (1992), for example, proposed that the art curricula and much of art education thinking in the public schools has been ethnocentric, which he states is an implicit part of racism. He follows LeVine's and Campbell's (1972) definition of ethnocentrism:

. . . a familiar word most generally understood, in parallel with "egocentrism," as an attitude or outlook in which values derived from one's own cultural background are applied to other cultural contexts where different values are operative. In the most naive form of ethnocentrism, termed "phenomenal absolutism" by Segall, Campbell, and Herskovits (1965), a person unreflectively takes his own culture values as objective reality and automatically uses them as the context within which he judges less familiar objects and events. It does not occur to such a person that there is more than one point of view. At a more complex level is the ethnocentric attitude or outlook that takes account of multiple points of view but regards those of other cultures as incorrect, inferior or immoral. (Segall, Campbell, & Herskovits, 1965, p. 134)

When displayed by a teacher providing instruction to students of differing cultural backgrounds, ethnocentrism can have devastating effects on those students' self-esteem and academic abilities. This form of racism diverts minority students' attention and interests from academic pursuits, making it more likely they will spend time and energy responding to the racism in nonproductive ways (Pollard, 1989). Pollard further asserts that some educators need to overcome their ethnocentrism and open themselves—and their students—to the achievements and experiences of other cultures.

Clark (1988) cites the following statement from the Supreme Court's famous *Brown v. Board of Education* (1954) decision that described some of the effects of segregation on Black children:

To separate them from others of similar age and qualifications solely because of their race generates a feeling of inferiority as to their status in the community that may affect their hearts and minds in a way unlikely ever to be undone. (*Brown v. Board of Education*, 1954, p. 34)

Clark (1988) documents another telling passage from the *Brown* decision:

A sense of inferiority affects the motivation of a child to learn. Segregation, with the sanction of law, therefore, has a tendency to retard the educational and mental development of Negro children and to deprive them of some of the benefits they would receive in a racially integrated school system. (*Brown v. Board of Education*, 1954, p. 36)

Concern about the negative effects of segregation and racism on the children of the majority race was documented in material related to the *Brown* decision, as well. Clark (1988) noted that in the Social Science Brief of the *Appendix to the Appellant's Briefs*, the social, psychological, and human value damage inflicted upon non-minority children was clearly summarized as follows:

Those children who learn the prejudices of our society are also being taught to gain personal status in an unrealistic and non-adaptive way. When comparing themselves to members of the minority group, they are not required to evaluate themselves in terms of the more basic standards of actual personal ability and achievement. The culture permits and, at times, encourages them to direct their feelings of hostility and aggression against whole groups of people the members of which are perceived as weaker than themselves. They often develop patterns of guilt feelings, rationalizations and other mechanisms which they must use in an attempt to protect themselves from recognizing the essential injustice of their unrealistic fears and hatreds of minority groups. (*Appendix to Appellant's Briefs*, 1952, p. 44)

The *Brown* decision resulted in widespread social change in American life. Its assertions of fundamental social and psychological truths cleared the way for the removal of all state laws that required or permitted racial discrimination and segregation in public accommodations, public transportation, and publicly supported recreational facilities. The *Brown* decision made it possible for Blacks to defy and remove the traditional signs of social humiliation and cruelties, and to educate White Americans in the importance of concern for the humanity of their fellow human beings without regard to color or race (Clark, 1988). Most important, the *Brown* decision provided explicit assertions of the damage that racism causes to students of all races.

Fortunately, many schools across the United States have educational programs and activities aimed at fostering ethnic awareness among students. Thomson (1989) asserts that building tolerance and understanding is important at each level of learning, including early childhood. She believes that young children learn best through hands-on experiences and through active involvement with materials and people. An early childhood teacher, Thomson has developed activities to help young children develop racial tolerance by "pretending to be Martin Luther King, Jr., in a bus boycott role-play, by choosing between the unknown contents of a beautiful box and a dirty carton, and by encountering discriminatory signs in a classroom activity" (p. 78). She states that the open-ended nature of these activities allows for queries from children as well as from teachers, and that both the activities and the queries encourage critical and creative thinking (Thomson, 1989). Educators' early efforts to intervene in students' lives in opposition to racism is an important initial step.

Concerns about their students' lack of ethnic awareness led two principals in Connecticut—one at a Black school in Hartford and the other at an all-White school in West Hartford—to collaborate. The principal in Hartford was concerned about racial isolation, while the principal in West Hartford feared that her students would accept the stereotypes of the past unless they really got to know some Black students (Foster, 1989). Together, they developed a project, "Across the Lines," with the purpose of bringing students from the two schools together. The student contacts focused on academics and opportunities for the students to study together. The school psychologist used an "imaging" study to assess students' attitudes and expectations. The findings showed that many Black students believed that they were perceived negatively by Whites in social and academic areas. Their fears were confirmed by the White students' self-reports. The Anglo students perceived Blacks as uniformly using poor grammar, showing bad manners, having low intelligence, wearing flashy clothes, living in project housing, and having no college plans (Foster, 1989).

Once the students from the two schools actually met, however, many found themselves to be pleasantly surprised by these encounters; most of the character flaws that they expected the other group to exhibit did not exist. The students acknowledged that some of the faults they had expected to find in the other group also existed in their own. Some Black students were still skeptical of the White students, but they felt they could enter a mostly White gathering with less apprehension than before (Foster, 1989). This exercise was instrumental in breaking down not only racial isolation, but also existing stereotypes. This kind of activity allows students to see firsthand how inhibiting stereotypes can be, as well as to see the number of commonalities that exist between races. Most important, this program allowed students to make their own decisions about individuals. As Dube (1985) asserted, children who see firsthand the contradiction between social stereotypes and reality are not likely to embrace those stereotypes.

Nikki Giovanni (1994), noted poet and professor of English at Virginia Polytechnic Institute and State University, offers advice to Black students in how to deal effectively with racism at predominantly White institutions. She offers some rules to follow that may help:

- *Go to class.* It is important to have a consistent presence in the classroom. If nothing else, the professor will know you care and are serious enough to be there.
- *Meet your professors.* Put them on notice that you are serious about getting good grades.
- *Do assignments on time.*
- *Go back to see your professor.* Ask early what you need to do if you feel you are starting to get into academic trouble.
- *Understand that there will be professors who do not like you.* There may even be professors who are racist or sexist, or both.
- *Don't defeat yourself.* Cultivate your friends. Know your enemies. You cannot

undo hundreds of years of prejudicial thinking. Think for yourself and speak up. Raise your hand in class. Say what you believe no matter how awkward you may think it sounds. You will improve in your articulation and confidence.
- *Participate in some campus activities.* Join the newspaper staff. Run for office. Join a dorm council. Do something that involves you on campus. You are going to be there for four years, so let your presence be known. (Giovanni, 1994, p. 20)

Although Giovanni's advice was specifically for Black students attending predominantly White institutions, these guidelines are applicable to all students. Educators themselves bear a crucial responsibility to address and reduce the impact of racism on students. School boards and superintendents of school districts can work actively to reduce racism by:

- Articulating a clear statement of expectations regarding racism (i.e., explaining that it will not be tolerated in any form)
- Establishing and enforcing a series of consequences for violations of those expectations
- Providing rewards for those who strive to reduce racism in their schools and classrooms. (Pollard, 1989, p. 73)

Pollard (1989) also lists a number of strategies for helping teachers mitigate racism in their classrooms:

- Teachers need to assess how they interpret the behavior of both minority and White students.
- Teachers should confront racist behavior, whether or not it is intentional.
- Teachers need to carefully monitor their own behavior. One way they can do this is to invite a friendly and honest colleague to observe classroom interactions, and then supply informal feedback.
- Finally, in assessing student performance, teachers need to be sure to give both minority and majority students encouragement, as well as specific suggestions about how to improve their academic work. (p. 74)

With regard to educators' specific role, Clark (1988) holds educators to a high standard. He asserts that a "truly educated person (specifically educators) must be prepared to assist his fellow human beings through empathy to attain and live by such uniquely human values as justice, kindness, and social sensibility" (p. 129). He further states that

. . . educators are aware of the fact that educational institutions dominated by race damage and dehumanize human beings. Those who remain silent in the face of these clear facts cannot be considered educators, but must be seen as accessories to the perpetuation of this damage on powerless human beings. (p. 130)

In an article addressing the continuing dilemma of racism in America, Molnar (1989) describes the role that schools have to play in this struggle against racism:

Schools have an important role to play in this struggle against racism. Schools are not sanctuaries. Schools can address the interpersonal aspects of racism as well as offer school and classroom activities that teach about the devastating effects oppression has had on minority group members and their cultures while at the same time acknowledging the strengths and contributions of minority group members and their cultures. (p. 72)

Administrators at predominantly Black institutions are expected to provide the same quality of education with far less funds. The level of institutionalized racism that creates barriers in education makes it almost impossible for many young people to enter teacher education programs. A minimum of a 2.7 GPA and successful earnings of 647 and 645 scores on the National Teacher Examination (NTE) are the deciding factors for entering teacher education programs. These become additional barriers for ill-prepared students, especially in some of the southern states, which are at the bottom of the list when education systems are evaluated. The education system in predominantly African American schools often is influenced by racism that affects relationships among teachers, counselors, and administrators. Some White educators do not understand the behavioral patterns or learning styles of African American students; therefore, they may view them as having learning deficits. Consequently, African American students often receive an education that does not adequately prepare them, intellectually or academically, to succeed in many teacher education programs.

Racism in education adversely affects not only students, but also society as a whole. Its effects and implications are expansive, but not irreversible. With a concerted effort from educators, students, administrators, legislators, and society, a shift towards racial equality and understanding can take place.

References

Appendix to the Appellant's Briefs. (1952). *The effect of segregation and the consequences of desegregation: A social science statement.*

Boyer, J., & Baptiste, H. P. (1996). *Transforming the curriculum for multicultural understandings: A practitioner's handbook.* San Francisco: Caddo Gap Press.

Brown, K. (1985). Turning a blind eye: Racial oppression and the unintended consequences of white non-racism. *Sociological Review, 33,* 670-690.

Brown vs. Board of Education, 347 U.S. 483 (1954).

Chalmers, F. (1992). The origins of racism in the public school art curriculum. *Studies in Art Education, 33*(3), 134-143.

Clark, K. (1988). The Brown decision: Racism, education, and human values. *Journal of Negro Education, 57*(2), 125-132.

Dube, E. (1985). The relationship between racism and education in South Africa. *Harvard Educational Review, 55*(1), 86-100.

Foster, L. (1989). Breaking down racial isolation. *Educational Leadership, 34*(2), 76-77.

Giovanni, N. (1994). Campus racism 101. *Academe, 21,* 19-20.

LeVine, R., & Campbell, D. (1972). *Ethnocentrism: Theories of conflict, ethnic attitudes and group behavior.* New York: John Wiley and Sons.

McCarthy, C. (1988). Rethinking liberal and radical perspectives in racial inequality in schooling: Making the case for nonsynchrony. *Harvard Educational Review, 58*(3), 265-279.

Molnar, A. (1989). Racism in America: A continuing dilemma. *Educational Leadership, 34*(2), 71-72.

Pollard, D. (1989). Reducing the impact of racism on students. *Educational Leadership, 34*(2), 73-75.

Segall, M., Campbell, D., & Herskovits, M. (1965). *The influence of culture on visual perception.* New York: Bobbs-Merrill.

Thomson, B. (1989). Building tolerance in early childhood. *Educational Leadership, 34*(2), 78-79.

Chapter II

History of Racism: Social, Political, and Psychological Perspectives on Modernity

H. Prentice Baptiste, Jr., *New Mexico State University*
James B. Boyer, Socorro Herrera, Kevin Murry,
Kansas State University

When writing this chapter, we decided to take a bold step in describing the history of racism in American society. We recognize that one can spend much time focusing on definitions of racism, and debating the significance of individual, institutional and cultural racism. As readers will discover, we are more intrigued with the historical, personal aspects of racism. Therefore, we have taken a critical look at racism's permanence in society; its sociocultural, political, and violent parameters; and its clandestine power to cause rage both in the abuser and the abused.

There is so much to be considered when one thinks of the historical dimensions of racism in the United States. The context for *this* discussion is limited to the relations of Black Americans and European (Caucasian) Americans because that context represents the origin of how race affects all activities—political, religious, educational, economic, and certainly any and all social activity.

It should be remembered, however, that racism was seldom discussed publicly in "the academy" by scholars, because so much of racism was either accepted or resignedly tolerated. In the United States, almost every decision connects itself in some way to the racial identity, the racial perspective, and the racial composition of any given community or interaction.

IN DENIAL OF RACISM

In many circles, both Black Americans and European (Caucasian) Americans are in denial about the powerful effect of race on everyday decisions and activities. This is because the term "racism" implies conflict, which sometimes becomes violent, even deadly. Since the 1950s, the word frequently has been used to indicate the uses and misuses of power in relations with other people. To be in denial allows one to escape, temporarily, certain realities. Some Americans, while attempting to engage in racial healing, do so without adequate diagnosis of the problem. In general, however, Americans appear to be re-awakening to the reality of racism in the United States, and researchers and scholars are beginning to address the ills, the diagnosis, and possible solutions.

What is racism? Why is it such an explosive concept? To what extent do we go to avoid accepting the term and all of its reflections? In general, racism is a way of thinking and behaving that assumes a person's value is determined by the color of his or her skin. Racists believe that intellect, social graces, even integrity and character, are measured along racial lines. Historically, this attitude has been reflected in American policies, programs, procedures, and activities. Both Black and non-Black Americans find it difficult to discuss such racism. Paul Kivel (1996), in *Uprooting Racism: How White People Can Work for Racial Justice*, offers the following:

Most of the time we don't notice or question our whiteness. However, when the subject is racism, many of us don't want to be white, because it opens us to charges of being racist and brings up feelings of guilt, shame, embarrassment, and hopelessness. There are others who proudly claim whiteness under any circumstances and simply deny or ignore the violence that white people have done to people of color. (p. 10)

Discussions of race and its implications tend to remain complex, even in these enlightened times. One must deal with the historical manifestations of racist thinking in order to comprehend how we got to the present manifestations. What does this mean in terms of our understanding of racism for the year 2000 and beyond? The harmful effects of racism in the United States can never be healed until racist thinking is directly addressed. Much of that thinking is influenced by what is learned in school.

ADDRESSING RACISM

As Kivel (1996) noted, discussions of racism often generate feelings of guilt, shame, hopelessness, and embarrassment. While this is regrettable, it may be necessary in order to begin the healing process. Therefore, addressing racism may be one of the most crucial actions that Americans can take, because racism's manifestations are so public and its reflections of power, prestige, and privilege are so visible.

Without offering a time frame, the following policies and practices reflect what once was part of everyday life in the United States.

- Many school districts across the United States paid African American teachers less of a salary than their Caucasian counterparts received—in the same school districts, serving under the same school board. Such salary schedules were published and were common knowledge.
- Some Whites-only schools would discard outdated textbooks, and give them to schools serving Black children; the White children would then receive new textbooks.
- It was once illegal to teach a Black person to read and write. In 1830, however, Prudence Crandall, a White teacher operating a school for White girls in Connecticut, secretly began teaching Black girls at night. When the townspeople learned what Crandall was doing, they burned down her school, socially ostracized her, and ran her out of town.
- Segregated schools were an accepted part of society for many years. Many Black children were transported past neighborhood schools, instead traveling long distances to reach schools designated for Black children. This meant, in some

instances, getting up earlier in the morning and returning much later in the afternoon. Furthermore, Black schools usually made do with limited resources and outdated materials.

- It was illegal for Blacks and Whites to sit in the same sections of buses, both city- and privately owned. Black Americans were required to sit in the back of the bus, even if there were only two or three White passengers. This situation led to the famous Montgomery, Alabama, bus boycott in 1955, initiated by the actions of Rosa Parks. Some historians mark that event as the beginning of the Civil Rights Movement.

- Even in neighborhoods populated largely by Black Americans, grocery stores and other places of business would not employ them except in custodial and similar roles. In the 1950s, Civil Rights leaders began to use such slogans as, "Don't buy where you can't work!" to alert policymakers, legislators, and the public that such a system could not continue unchallenged.

- Employment opportunities for African Americans were severely limited in a way that they were not for White Americans.

- The privilege of eating in a restaurant, even in national chains like Howard Johnson's, was denied to African Americans. Some restaurants would serve Blacks, but only if they went to the back door. While the cooks and chefs were often African American, they were not allowed to sit in the customer sections of the establishments in which they worked.

- African Americans were not allowed to be seated at soda fountains in drug stores. Once could buy an ice cream cone while standing at the cash register, but could not be seated on stools at the counter. This was dramatically challenged in 1960 when African American college students staged a sit-in at local stores in Greensboro, North Carolina.

- Most African Americans were denied the right to register and vote, until passage of the Voting Rights of 1965. Some states established a literacy test for all persons not already registered. It was illogical and difficult beyond description, and was used only when Black Americans attempted to register. At the same time, African Americans paid the same taxes and prices.

RACISM: A MENTALITY

These examples of racism's manifestations represent just a small sample of the policies, procedures, and practices once prevalent in the United States. This history is alarmingly recent. It is no wonder that the healing process requires dialogue on what such practices meant. Racism's impact on society still haunts us all.

Given such powerful, long-standing manifestations of a "superior-inferior" model, the mentality will require a major overhaul in order for authentic healing to occur. Dialogue about racism and its manifestations must be part of the intervention and part of the correction.

A CHRONOLOGY OF RACIAL HATRED IN THE UNITED STATES

Several outcomes are possible when differing racial groups come into contact. Although both extremes of relationships—completely harmonious integration, or complete disruption without integration—are possible, Schermerhorn (1970) reminds us that either end of the extreme is rare, and that some sort of dialectical relationship is more likely. Such relationships are more often than not characterized by overlapping processes of conflict and integration (a process whereby societal elements are brought into compliance with those of the group whose norms are most embraced by society), or of conflict and accommodation. If two racial groups in contact maintain separate group identities and coexist in an environment where intergroup competition is possible, then the potential exists for the development of differential power—that which favors a particular group over another (Wilson, 1973).

With the attainment of differential power, the dominant group is in a position to force its values, interests, and cultural norms upon the subordinate group. This is particularly true if the dominant group is also able to publicly demean the subordinate group (Blumer, 1958). Original contact among racial groups is typically of three types, each with its own particular implications for the attainment of a differential power base (Wilson, 1973). Slave transfers, a situation experienced by most Blacks in Colonial and Postcolonial America, constitute a contact situation in which the dominant group has supreme power over the subordinate population. Colonization, the second form of contact, entails a nonindigenous racial group gaining control of a given territory. The experiences of both Native Americans and Mexican Americans probably best typify this type of contact. Colonization carries with it the second most powerful potential for domination via differential power. The third type of contact is voluntary migration, which, although it is associated with the greatest degree of freedom of choice and movement, often has meant exploitation and discrimination of the migrating group by the receiving dominant group. The experiences of Asian Americans in the United States provide a compelling example of this type of contact.

This chronology focuses on selected, but representative, aspects of the experiences of four subordinate, racial groups in the United States. Their interracial histories are indicative of the three broad types of first contact. Concomitantly, this chronology illustrates the sort of hatred and rage that may arise when contact between racial groups is demonstrative of an existent or emergent differential power base.

Finally, we have attempted to lend a somewhat analytical bend to the chronology by exploring five eras of race relations among these groups in the United States, as well as three perspectives within each of these eras. The sociopolitical perspective examines key legislative, legal, and political milestones. The sociocultural perspective explores selected benchmarks that are indicative of prevailing societal ideologies, value systems, norms, or practices. The sociohistorical perspective details key events that enable a comparison of race relations across eras.

The Era of Emergent Subordination {1600-1861}

Since this era encompasses the founding of the Jamestown Colony, the passage of the Indian Removal Bill, the signing of the Treaty of Guadalupe Hidalgo, and the Passenger Cases of 1849, no other era of the chronology is more associated with the nature and characteristics of first contact. Moreover, slave transfers, colonization, and voluntary migration each existed within this time period. Hence, the era can be referred to as the Era of Emergent Subordination.

Sociopolitical perspective
{1600-1861}:

- **1690**—To ensure swift and severe justice, Carolina, as Virginia has already done creates special courts for slaves through the Slave Code of 1690. When called before these tribunals, slaves did not receive a trial by jury. Additionally, only three of the court's five members were needed to convict slaves of crimes punishable by death.

- **1787**—In the Three-Fifths Compromise, Congress provides that three-fifths of a state's slave population may be counted for the purpose of calculating both a state's representation and its taxes.

- **1793**—According to the provisions of the Fugitive Slave Act passed by Congress, masters or their agents may seize a Black person in order to prove ownership before any state or federal judge. The Black person, on the other hand, has no right to a trial by jury, nor any right to testify or to present witnesses. The law virtually legalizes the kidnapping of Black persons in the United States.

- **1830**—Despite the reaffirmation of the Royal Proclamation (1763) by the Continental Congress (1778), Native Americans are effectively denied their property, rights, and liberty through passage of the Indian Removal Bill, which mandates that all Native Americans move west of the Mississippi River.

- **1848**—The Treaty of Guadalupe-Hidalgo, consummated on February 2, is the final chapter of the Mexican American War. The United States does not send a high-ranking diplomat to the negotiations, but merely a chief clerk from the State Department. The U.S. government, in acquiring approximately one-half of Mexico's pre-independence holdings in the West, assumes responsibility for thousands of Mexicans living within those boundaries. These people are given the unenviable choice of either leaving the conquered territory (and all their possessions) within one year or becoming American citizens by default. Thus, with the exception of the Native Americans, Mexicans become the only subordinate group in the United States annexed by conquest.

- **1849**—In the first legislation to play a major role in shaping the history of Asian Americans, the U.S. Supreme Court rules that immigration is, constitutionally, foreign commerce, and therefore may be limited by an act of Congress. Nativist politicians strive to curb foreign influence in American life.

- **1850**—The State of California enacts the Foreign Miner's License Tax Act, a tax originally aimed at Latin Americans, which comes to have a greater impact on Asian miners, who are charged four dollars per month to work in the gold mines. By 1869, Chinese miners have paid 85 percent of the state's total revenue from this tax.

- **1854**—In *People v. Hall*, the California Supreme Court rules 2 to 1 that a White man charged with murder has been wrongly convicted because Chinese witnesses have testified against him. The inadmissibility of their evidence, according to the decision, is covered by the proscription on testimony by Blacks and Indians in the California State Constitution.

- **1860**—The House Commerce Committee's Report on the "Cooke Trade" becomes one of the earliest calls, at the government level, for Chinese exclusion.

Sociocultural perspective
{1600-1861}:

- **1640**—Uprooted from their native societies, Black arrivals find themselves in an unfamiliar land with little culture or language in common among themselves. Therefore, they are not able to effectively resist White authority. Furthermore, the prevailing prejudice against those of dark skin enables Whites to justify slavery. Those of European ancestry are first convinced that the Blacks are "heathen," then persuaded that African societies are backward, barbarous, and therefore inferior to White societies. By 1661, Virginia's Assembly has begun to legally recognize the notion of lifetime servitude.

- **1831**—The Turner Rebellion, attributed to a literate slave who had drawn inspiration from the Bible, promulgated the belief that literate bonded servants are more likely to be troublemakers than illiterate ones. By 1835, five Southern states have outlawed teaching slaves to read or write. During the 1830s, the only two Southern states still permitting free Blacks to vote withdraw that right.

- **1848**—Primarily provoked by the annexation of Texas, the Mexican-American War represents the culmination of three decades of sociocultural conflict in Texas. To the Mexicans, every incident in Texas, from the filibustering raids to the revolution in 1836, comes to be regarded as part of a deliberately planned scheme of conquest. Moreover, the way in which the United States conducts the war adds greatly to the resulting heritage of hatred. Murder, robbery, and the rape of women in the presence of their families are among the atrocities committed by volunteer soldiers.

- **1850**—Reservations, established as a means of forced segregation, become the new reality of life for Native Americans.

- **1852**—The antislavery novel *Uncle Tom's Cabin*, written by Harriet Beecher Stowe, vividly depicts the horrors of slavery in America. Its phenomenal success in the North fuels Southern hostility toward the North.

- **1857**—The gap between the North and the South is widened by the Supreme Court's famous *Dred Scott v. Sanford* decision, in which the court maintains that the U.S. Constitution, when drafted, had not considered Blacks in that they had been socially regarded as "so far inferior, that they had no rights which the White man was bound to respect." Therefore, the court concludes, Blacks should not be considered as U.S. citizens.

Sociohistorical and racial violence perspective
{1600-1861}:

- **1609**—Jamestown, Virginia: John Smith initiates military raids against nearby Native American villages, looting them for food and other supplies to sustain his failing colony.

- **1643**—New Amsterdam: Dutch soldiers raid Wecquaesgeek settlements, murdering and mutilating Indians of both sexes and all ages. Officers report seeing infants dismembered and burned. Corpses are mutilated to such an extent that civilians initially blame hostile Indians for the massacre.

- **1676**—Boston: Nipmuck leader Sagamore John surrenders 180 members of his tribe to colonists. As a sign of good faith, the Nipmucks are required to execute their own sachem, Matoonas, and his son on Boston Common.

- **1730**—Williamsburg, Virginia: Several slaves are sentenced to "severe whippings" after they hold meetings to discuss their possible freedom. Six weeks later, four abolitionist spokesmen are executed.

- **1768**—Middle Creek, Pennsylvania: Frederick Stump, a German settler, murders six Indians at his home and conceals their bodies in a creek; the next day, he kills four more in their village in order to prevent news of the murders from spreading.

- **1816**—Negro Fort, Florida: U.S. Troops under Gen. Andrew Jackson destroy a fortified settlement of runaway slaves and Seminole Indians in Spanish territory. A total of 270 men, women, and children are killed. News of the massacre is suppressed by Washington, but it becomes the trigger incident for a full-scale war with the Seminoles.

- **1830-1843**—Except for the Iroquois and Seminole, over 100,000 Native Americans are forcibly removed from their lands; about 12,000 die on the "Trail of Tears."

- **1850**—Yuma County, Arizona: John Glanton and his gang of professional scalp hunters are surrounded and annihilated by Yuma Indians. Authorities conclude that Glanton's pack of "border scum" slaughtered at least 1,000 Indians in the past two years, which earned them an estimated $100,000 selling scalps.

- **1853**—California records more homicides than all other states combined during this year, with the majority of victims listed as Mexicans or Indians killed by Whites.

- **1855**—Leavenworth, Kansas: William Phillips, a free-soil attorney working to have November's pro-slavery vote overturned on grounds of fraud, is seized by a mob that shaves his head, coats him with tar and feathers, and then "sells" him in a mock slave auction.

- **1857**—Texas: Anglo settlers launch a systematic campaign of terrorism designed to force Mexican American traders out of the lucrative transportation business between San Antonio and Chihuahua, Mexico. This so-called "cart war" will rage for more than a year.

The Era of Manifest Destiny
{1862-1940}

In a mid-19th century issue of *United States Magazine and Democratic Review,* an anonymous author defended the annexation of Texas, while upholding "our manifest destiny to overspread the continent allotted by Providence for the free development of our multiplying millions" (as quoted in Jatras, 1997). In the years that would follow, this belief in the inherent superiority of dominant Western cultural values, including the desire to conquer and exploit the environment, would become the foundation for racial conflict in the United States, especially as it concerned Native Americans, Asian Americans, and Mexican Americans.

Sociopolitical perspective
{1862-1940}:

- **1863**—President Abraham Lincoln signs the Emancipation Proclamation, which he characterizes not as an act of liberation but rather as a military necessity. The proclamation serves as an open invitation for approximately 3 million slaves in Confederate territory to cross over to Union lines. The joy and celebration among Northern Blacks is epitomized by the eloquence of one such man:

Once, the time was that I cried all night. What's the matter? What's the matter? Matter enough. The Next Morning my child was to be sold, and she was sold; and I never 'pected to see her no more til the day of judgment. Now, no more that! No More That! With my hands against my breast I was going to my work, when the overseer used to whip me along. Now, no more that! No more that! No more that! (Quoted in LeVine, 1996).

- **1871**—The U.S. Congress passes an appropriations bill rider mandating that Native American tribes are no longer independent nations. Legislation, not negotiation, determines any new arrangements with Native Americans.
- **1882**—The Chinese Exclusion Act, first vetoed by President Arthur, is passed; it bars all Chinese immigration for at least 10 years. It is the first time the federal government has enacted a human embargo on a particular race of laborers. After racial violence in Los Angeles (1871), which leaves 21 Chinese dead, and in Rock Springs, Wyoming (1885), which leaves 28 Chinese dead and many others wounded, Congress will renew the Chinese Exclusion Act for another 10 years in 1892 and extend it indefinitely in 1902.
- **1887**—The Dawes Act mandates that Native American reservations are to be subdivided in tracts and allotted to individual tribal members, while so-called "surplus" land is to be sold.
- **1889**—The Curtis Act terminates tribal governments among Native Americans who refuse allotment. Instead, the President will appoint tribal chiefs hereafter.
- **1896**—The United States Supreme Court, in *Plessy v. Ferguson*, bases its ruling regarding a Louisiana railroad segregation law on a "separate but equal" doctrine, which holds that segregation is constitutional if equal facilities are provided for Blacks. Ultimately, this decision paves the way for a proliferation of so-called "Jim Crow" segregationist legislation, especially in the Southern states.
- **1898**—In *Williams v. Mississippi*, the U.S. Supreme Court promulgates growing efforts toward the disenfranchisement of African Americans by declaring that the poll tax and literacy requirements for voting are constitutional. At this time, public opinion is profoundly influenced by a new, pseudoscientific "Social Darwinism," which proclaims Blacks to be inferior by nature, and therefore unchangeable.
- **1902-1920**—A series of enactments known as Anti-Alien Land Laws are passed by several Far Western States and are typified by the California Anti-Alien Land Law of 1920. The laws limit the right of Asian Americans to own land, compounding pressure upon people who have already been denied citizenship.
- **1906**—The Burke Act eliminates the right of Native Americans to lease their land, with the intent of forcing Native Americans to work the land themselves.
- **1908**—A race riot one-half mile from the Illinois home of Abraham Lincoln spawns a spree of atrocities against Blacks, including property destruction, flogging, and lynching. In response to the violence, a group of Blacks and a growing

number of liberal Whites call for a series of meetings designed to renew the struggle for civil and political liberty. At the second of these meetings, on May 12-14, 1910, the National Association for the Advancement of Colored People (NAACP) is established.

- **1915**—The NAACP fights to prevent the public showing of D. W. Griffith's "Birth of a Nation," which depicts Reconstruction as an attempt by barbaric Blacks to take over the South and have their way with White women; Ku Klux Klan members are depicted as heroes for having saved the South from this fate.
- **1934**—Forty-seven years after Native Americans were denied their property rights by the Dawes Act, the U.S. Government recants and ends the Allotment Program via the Indian Reorganization Act.

Sociocultural perspective
{1862-1940}:

- **1846-1896**—Although many United States citizens see the Mexican Annexation that followed the Treaty of Guadalupe-Hidalgo as a fulfillment of Manifest Destiny, for the newly created Mexican Americans it is an experience of economic subjugation, followed by ethnic prejudice and discrimination. This group suffers not only the psycho-historical experience of a rapid and violent break with a parent country culture, but also forced subjugation. All of this takes place on what this indigenous population considers to be its own land. As McLemore and Romo (1985) point out, these and other factors render the Mexican American experience different from that of all other racial groups that migrate to this part of North America in the 19th and 20th centuries; it is what some have called the ultimate violence.
- **1849-1902**—What began as isolated, regional violence against Asian Americans in the West builds into national discrimination with the Passage of the Chinese Exclusion Act of 1892. According to Daniels (1988), national opinion, pervaded by racism, burgeons into a generalized feeling of ethnic superiority among Whites, characterized by a surprising level of unanimity among the White majority in favor of everything anti-Chinese.
- **1866**—Following the Civil War, White terrorist gangs emerge throughout the South. The Ku Klux Klan, founded in Tennessee, is primarily composed of poor Whites, who wear white hoods and robes amidst their acts of terror. Blacks are a favorite target, especially those considered "impudent" toward Whites, those who are well educated, or any others thought not to "know their place."
- **1887-1906**—Shifts in government policy during this time period are profoundly influenced by a generalized desire among Whites to impose the tenets of the western cultural canon upon Native Americans, especially the value of rugged individualism. This desire is exemplified by the General Allotment Act of 1887. Its sponsor, Senator Dawes, naively believes that it will change the Native American from an individual who values the cooperative, noncompetitive approach, to one who cherishes that spirit of self-interest that he, and others like him, consider the major force in White civilization.
- **1889-1899**—Lynching becomes the most common form of racial violence perpe-

trated against African Americans during this time period. From 1889-1899, approximately 104 Blacks are lynched per year in the South; 23 per year are lynched in the North. "Convicted" of crimes without due process, victims are commonly hung from trees and are frequently castrated. Among the generally suspect justifications given for lynching are the need to protect White women from Black rapists; allegations of murder; suspicion of robbery; and many non-crimes, including trying to vote, testifying in court, or failing to call a White man "mister."

- **1917**—The ebbing tide of immigration from Europe, a consequence of World War I, prompts the unprecedented, large-scale migration of southern African Americans into northern industrial centers such as Chicago. Racial clashes are increasingly frequent, especially when Blacks are used as strikebreakers. One of the worst clashes occurs in East St. Louis, Illinois, where the African American population has nearly tripled (from 6,000 to 16,000) as a consequence of the war effort. On July 1, White joyriders randomly fire shots into Black homes and churches. When two of the riders are killed in retaliatory attacks, a four-day riot ensues in which White mobs storm Black neighborhoods, randomly attacking men, women, and children. In the end, over one-half of the Black population flee the city, and more than 100 are shot, mutilated, and beaten.

Sociohistorical and racial violence perspective {1862-1940}:

- **1864**—Ft. Canby, New Mexico: The first party of defeated Navajo begin their "long walk" to confinement at Ft. Sumner. By May 11, 4,776 men, women, and children will make the overland trek, with soldiers recording 320 deaths along the way. Another 126 are reported dead in captivity.
- **1864**—Ft. Pillow, Tennessee: Rebel troops under Gen. Nathan Bedford Forest, later Grand Wizard of the KKK, capture the Union garrison. Black Union troops, women, and children are executed in various ways: some are crucified, some are burned at the stake, and some are buried alive "as a lesson" to other Blacks serving the North.
- **1870**—York County, South Carolina: Klan nightriders launch a terror campaign lasting through September 1871. Best estimates indicate at least 11 murders and 600 serious beatings occurred. Five Black schools and churches are destroyed.
- **1873**—Lincoln, Mew Mexico: Constable Juan Martinez dies in a gun battle with the Harrell clan, a band of racist marauders. When three members of the gang are killed, the others raid the town, killing four Mexican Americans. U.S. troops chase the marauders out of town, but they stop long enough to execute Jose Haskell for the "crime" of marrying a Mexican American woman.
- **1875**—Texas: Thirty-two Texas Rangers illegally cross the border into Mexico, assaulting a ranch suspected of harboring Mexican troops. No soldiers are found, but the Rangers massacre innocent civilians, covering their error by naming the victims "bandits."
- **1879**—Bee County, Texas: Congressional investigators report that Whites have brutally murdered a Mexican American man "because he would not go and play fiddle for them."
- **1881**—Denver, Colorado: An argument between a White man and two Chinese

men sparks an anti-Chinese riot by 3,000 Whites. A Chinese laundryman, Sing Lee, is lynched, and more than 100 Chinese are jailed "for their own protection." Sing Lee's lynchers are acquitted by a jury four months later.

- **1883**—Pierce City, Idaho: Merchant D. M. Frazier is found dead in his shop. Vigilantes seize two Chinese competitors, torturing both until each accuses the other of Frazier's murder. That night, a White mob lynches the two suspects, along with three other "undesirable" Chinese. The incident triggers a wholesale expulsion of Chinese from Idaho settlements.

- **1890**—Wounded Knee, South Dakota: Shooting breaks out after U.S. troops discover hidden weapons on the Sioux Reservation. In the resultant massacre, soldiers fire on 350 Native American men, women, and children, leaving 153 dead. Many others crawl away to die alone, and only 51 survivors are identified.

- **1896**—San Antonio, Texas: Aureliano Castellon is shot eight times, and his body burned by "persons unknown." He has been courting an Anglo girl, over the objections of her parents and brothers.

- **1916**—Waco, Texas: Jesse Washington, a mentally retarded Black youth, sentenced to hang for killing a White woman, is dragged from the courtroom by a mob, stabbed, mutilated, and burned alive while police stand and watch. The victim's teeth are later sold as souvenirs.

- **1920**—Ft. Worth, Texas: Pedro Torres, a Mexican American youth, is arrested and beaten by police for allegedly stealing two pairs of trousers. Tried as an adult despite the fact that he is underage and speaks no English, Torres is sentenced to serve five years in state prison.

- **1921**—Tulsa, Oklahoma: Dick Rowland, a 19-year-old African American, is jailed and charged with attempted rape after he steps on the foot of Sara Page, a White 43-year-old divorcee, and then stumbles and falls on her. A racial disturbance breaks out in which at least 150 African Americans are killed. Thirty Whites are later charged with looting, and a grand jury indicts seven civilians and five policeman—including the chief of police—on criminal charges linked to the riot.

- **1934**—Mississippi: National Guard units are called to protect three Black rape suspects. The defendants plead guilty one day later and are sentenced to die. One month later, state legislators pass a bill permitting the rape victim's father to hang her attackers. The execution is carried out 9 days later.

The Era of Separate But Unequal
{1941-1963}

Although the press for societal change is begun in earnest during Franklin Delano Roosevelt's administration, civil rights advocates later sense a small but momentous victory when, in a unanimous ruling, the U.S. Supreme Court in *Brown v. Board of Education of Topeka* declares that "separate educational facilities are inherently unequal" and, accordingly, violate the Fourteenth Amendment of the U.S. Constitution. This 60-year belated reversal of *Plessy v. Ferguson* (1896), however, is only weakly supported by the Eisenhower administration, which tends to take a hands-off policy toward defiance of the ruling. In fact, no real action is taken at the national or state levels to implement the spirit of the ruling until the advent of the civil rights marches years later.

Sociopolitical perspective
{1941-1963}:

- **1941-1943**—After the attack on Pearl Harbor, Executive Orders 9066 and 8972 authorize the internment of Japanese Americans in so-called relocation centers in Arkansas, Arizona, California, Colorado, Idaho, Utah, and Wyoming.

- **1942-1964**—The Bracero Program brings Mexican aliens into the United States on a temporary basis each year until harvests are completed. The system provides much-needed, low-cost labor to agriculturalists without the accompanying cost of educating the laborers' children.

- **1952**—The federal government's Relocation Program moves Native Americans, at government expense, to urban areas, on the premise of better job opportunities.

- **1953**—The Federal Termination Act authorizes the elimination of the reservation systems, with an immediate termination of federal services and tax immunity.

- **1954**—The U.S. Supreme Court in *Brown v. Board of Education of Topeka* declares that "separate educational facilities are inherently unequal" and, as such, they violate the Fourteenth Amendment of the U.S. Constitution.

- **1957**—When administering literacy tests to voting applicants, southern registrars often ask Whites simple questions, while asking Blacks impossible ones, such as "How many bubbles are in a bar of soap?" (LeVine, 1996). Although the Civil Rights Act of 1957 enables the Justice Department to sue registrars who discriminate among voters, the maximum penalty is a mere $300 fine or 45 days in jail.

Sociocultural perspective
{1941-1963}:

- **1941-1945**—African Americans who volunteer for military service in World War II soon discover that discrimination remains rampant in the ranks of the U.S. armed services. They receive inferior, segregated training in separate units. As the war proceeds, less than one percent of them will become commissioned officers. Particularly unconscionable is the Red Cross's decision to segregate the donated blood of Blacks and Whites. By 1943, the rage against segregation and discrimination in the armed forces reaches a climax. Riots break out in Beaumont, Texas; Los Angeles; and Detroit.

- **1953-1954**—The series of bills passed during this time period that end federal responsibility for Native Americans do not stipulate federal support for such services as medical care, schools, and road maintenance. Tribes such as the Menominee of Wisconsin are forced to sell choice property at bargain prices in order to maintain critical services. These termination statutes affect 109 tribes, 13,263 Native Americans, and over 1.3 million acres of trust land (Grobsmith & Ritter, 1992). For the small Klamath tribe, the termination statutes threaten to end their tribal identity.

- **1955**—The atmosphere of paranoia and intimidation fostered by Sen. Joseph McCarthy's crusade against communism and subversives at home severely weakens the cause of Civil Rights. Yet, less than a year after *Brown v. Board of Education of Topeka*, a seemingly isolated incident lays the foundation for the battle to come. On December 1, 1955, a Black seamstress, Rosa Parks, refuses to give up her seat to a

White man on a Montgomery, Alabama, public bus. Within four days, Blacks have begun to boycott the bus system. The leader of the boycott, Martin Luther King, Jr., displays an extraordinary brand of leadership that will set the tone for African American commitment to social justice for the next 10 years.

Sociohistorical and racial violence perspective {1941-1963}:

- **1941**—United States: Of the approximately 127,000 Japanese living in the United States at this time, 94,000 are in California, about 63 percent are U.S. born, and only 15 percent are of voting age. The U.S. response to these civilians following the December 7 attack on Pearl Harbor will come to be referred to as "our worst wartime mistake" (Rostow, 1945). More than 110,000 Japanese, many of them second- and third-generation Americans, are summarily removed from their homes, denied their property rights, and relocated to various internment centers throughout the Southwest. The evacuation will bring financial ruin to many of these Japanese American families; they will lose their property, savings, income, and jobs, for which they will not be adequately compensated.

- **1943**—Los Angeles: Two events on June 3 trigger the infamous Zoot Suit Riot. First, several Mexican American boys returning from a police-sponsored club meeting are assaulted by Whites from the same Los Angeles neighborhood. That same evening, 11 sailors on leave are attacked; they maintain that their assailants were Mexican youths who outnumbered them 3 to 1. In the five days that follow, rioting service-men and civilians attack Mexican Americans and Blacks, singling out youths who wear zoot suits for special attention. The violence peaks on June 7, when more than 1,000 rioters invade theaters, streetcars, and homes, dragging Mexican American youths out to be stripped and beaten. Police take little action, confining their arrests to battered victims of the mob. Ultimately, more than 600 Mexican Americans are jailed in a series of "preventive" arrests.

- **1944**—Amite County, Mississippi: Angered by the refusal of an African American minister, Isaac Simmons, to sell his oil-rich land, Whites abduct him and shoot him to death. Later, they break his bones and cut out his tongue. The minister's son is also beaten and directed to leave the county.

- **1948**—Los Angeles, California: In the midst of having a drink at a local pub, patrol-man William Keyes and his partner arrest a 17-year-old Mexican American, Augustino Salcido, bring him to a vacant building, and riddle his body with bullets. The officers testify that Augustino was selling stolen watches, but none are found at the scene. Later, police beat witnesses to the incident and force them out of town. In a subsequent trial, Keyes is acquitted on manslaughter charges.

- **1955**—Money, Mississippi: A 14-year-old African American boy, Emmett Till, is alleged to have whistled at a White man's wife. He is kidnapped, shot, and dumped in a river by local White vigilantes. His killers, who are acquitted by a local jury, later sell their confessions to a national magazine.

- **1960**—Austin, Texas: A bomb is detonated outside a building where members of the Texas University Religious Council are holding a meeting about the integration of local restaurants.

- **1963**—Mississippi: Three African Americans, including a woman, are found dead in their car, 10 miles outside of Woodville. Although the local press attributes their death to carbon monoxide poisoning, an African American undertaker reports finding broken bones and gunshot wounds in the bodies.
- **1963**—Alabama: Martin Luther King's campaign of civil disobedience against the evils of segregation, epitomized by the conditions in Birmingham, Alabama, is met with police dogs and fire hoses with pressure sufficient to tear the bark from trees. King, one of over 400 African Americans who are arrested, writes his famous "Letter from a Birmingham Jail." The protest comes on the heels of an inaugural speech by Governor George Wallace, who demands: "Segregation now! Segregation tomorrow! Segregation forever!"

The Era of Hopeful Disenchantment {1964-1980}

The early successes of nonviolent civil rights activists such as Martin Luther King, Ralph Abernathy, and Bob Moses do much to lift the hopes of African Americans. Nonetheless, by the mid-1960s, a growing number of African Americans have become disenchanted with the goal of integration and with King's strategy of nonviolence. Many of those who have lost faith in civil disobedience maintain that to pursue integration is to abandon their own identity. LeVine's (1996) reflections on this situation are noteworthy:

They believed that blacks must go beyond the two major strategies being used to attack racism. . . . The legal strategy assumed that the nation's judicial system was basically fair; the direct action strategy assumed that the consciences of whites could be moved. But the new black voices rejected both assumptions . . . [they] argued that blacks must 'use any means necessary,' including violence, to defeat racism. (p. 195)

At the same time, many Americans, especially White liberals, are shocked as these new Blacks find their voice. They find the apparent progress of African Americans to be irreconcilable with the anger and calls for violence. It seemingly does not occur to these Americans that long-oppressed groups often expect to realize rapid change in society once they find tangible evidence of hope. When such change is not the norm, frustration, disenchantment, and bitterness often result.

Sociopolitical perspective {1964-1980}:

- **1964-1965**—Celebration among African Americans in response to the passage of the Civil Rights Act of 1964 and the Voting Rights Act of 1965 is tempered by the news that three civil rights workers, Michael Schwerner, James Chaney, and Andrew Goodman, have been arrested for speeding, turned over to a waiting gang of Klansmen, murdered, and buried in an earthen dam outside of Philadelphia, Mississippi. Equally unconscionable is the state's refusal to file murder charges.
- **1968**—The Bilingual Education Act federally funds, but does not mandate, bilingual educational programs for Mexican American, Asian American, and other students whose English proficiency may be limited.

• **1974**—The U.S. Supreme Court's ruling in *Lau v. Nichols* is a political victory for non-English-speaking students, especially those who are of Asian or Mexican descent, in that it stipulates that special language programs are necessary for such students. In a more practicable sense, however, the ruling is a disappointment in that it not only falls short of mandating bilingual education, but also fails to specify specific guidelines by which school districts must abide in the equitable education of these students.

Sociocultural perspective
{1964-1980}:

• **1966-1969**—The victories of the civil rights movement in the South are less effective in the North, where the force of segregation was never as potent and African Americans have long been free to vote. The major problems of northern Blacks, including poverty, unemployment, and housing discrimination, are more difficult to ameliorate than voting discrimination and Jim Crow laws. Moreover, the North's efforts to integrate schools are viewed by many as inadequate and convince others that northern Whites are hypocritical concerning racial questions.

• **Late 1960s**—The gradual emergence of Black Power groups and increasing rhetoric favorable toward Black nationalism fosters dissension within the civil rights movement. What LeVine (1996) has termed a "White backlash" also begins to emerge as Senate debate gradually weakens the force and range of the Fair Housing Act in 1966, and the favorable mood of Congress toward civil rights legislation reaches its zenith in this era.

• **1973**—The efforts of the American Indian Movement to draw public attention to the plight of Native Americans via their 71-day siege of the village of Wounded Knee, South Dakota, enjoy only limited success. All charges against leaders of the movement are dropped and the FBI and Justice Department are severely criticized for their handling of the incident. Any hopes that the government would negotiate with the Sioux on the basis of an 1868 treaty that guaranteed them dominion over the northern plains, however, are not realized.

Sociohistorical and racial violence perspective
{1964-1980}:

• **1965**—Selma, Alabama: Authorities underestimate the power of the media in confrontations with civil rights demonstrators who have planned a march from Selma to Montgomery, the capital of Alabama. The marchers begin crossing the bridge from the Selma side. They are ordered to return to Selma but refuse to turn around. Subsequently, troops charge the crowd, and begin beating and trampling the demonstrators, who now begin fleeing toward Selma. An outraged nation watches the events of "Bloody Sunday" on television. Fourteen days later, the march, led by Martin Luther King, is resumed, 50,000 strong; this time, they have federal protection.

• **1966**—Chicago, Illinois: Martin Luther King underestimates the extent of racial hatred and bigotry in the North as he begins a series of marches in Chicago to demand integrated housing. Angry and violent White mobs greet the protesters with Confederate flags and swastikas; bricks, bottles, and rocks are hurled at the marchers.

- **1968**—Memphis, Tennessee: While waiting to lead a march in support of Black sanitation workers, Martin Luther King is assassinated, sparking riots in more than 100 U.S. cities.

- **1973**—Dallas, Texas: Santos Rodriquez, a 12-year-old Mexican American, is "accidentally" shot in the head by a policeman trying to extort a confession to a robbery. In the ensuing riot, 4 people are injured and 12 are arrested. The officer is later convicted of "murder without malice," and given a 5-year prison sentence.

- **1974**—Delano, California: Members of the Teamsters Union muscle their way into the fields, threatening both grape growers and members of the United Farm Workers of America (UFW), led by Cesar Chavez and Larry Itliong. Growers are persuaded to sign so-called "sweetheart" contracts with the Teamsters, which threaten the survival of the UFW.

- **1975**—Boston, Massachusetts: Six African American Bible salesmen are attacked by a crowd of approximately 100 Whites, some armed with baseball bats. Two of the 100 Whites are arrested on charges of assault with a deadly weapon. In the two months that follow, 98 people are arrested and 17 are injured in racial clashes in and around the Carson Beach area.

- **1978**—Houston, Texas: Two patrolmen are convicted of negligent homicide in the death of a Mexican American prisoner, J. C. Compos. One day later, they are each fined $1 and released on probation.

- **1980**—Youngstown, Ohio: As they walk home from a party, two African American girls are fired upon by White gunmen; both narrowly escape injury. Then, as the gunmen round a nearby street corner, they fire upon two African American adults. Veronica Vaughn is killed.

The Era of Civil Rights Retrenchment
{1980-Present}

Increasing retrenchment from the ideals of equity and equality is epitomized in the debate over the direction of American public school education. The 1980s witnessed a resurgence of assimilationist arguments under the guise of new catchwords such as "excellence" and "effectiveness." Generally, these proposals for reform advocate curricula heavily grounded in the tenets of the Western cultural canon, including a return to the classics. President Reagan, for instance,

. . . claimed that one reason that the schools were failing was the attention that had been focused on female, minority, and handicapped students. He asserted that, if the federal government and educators had not been so preoccupied with the needs of these special groups of students, education in the U.S. might not have succumbed to the "rising tide of mediocrity." What the president failed to note is that, if these three groups of students are eliminated only about 15 percent of the school population remains. (Shakeshaft, 1986, p. 499)

Although the attitude of the Clinton administration toward equity and equality (as evidenced by the administration's defense of affirmative action) in the 1990s has been more favorable than that of the Reagan and Bush administrations, retrenchment ideologies in Congress continue to block significant progress toward civil rights and more diversified, culturally sensitive curricula in the public schools.

Recent research (Herrera, 1996; Murry, 1996) uncovered demonstrable, longitudinal evidence that many K-12 public school educators in the Southwest and in the Midwest hold deeply ingrained, persistent, and racist attitude orientations toward their students of color, especially Vietnamese American, Native American, African American, and Mexican American students. Two of these racist orientations are especially noteworthy, and are best described as "meaning perspectives" (Mezirow, 1991). Meaning perspectives constitute a habitual set of expectations providing an orienting frame of reference or perceptual filter on experience.

The first of these meaning perspectives noted among public school educators is that of colorblind, nonaccommodative denial. Analysis of educators' discourse indicated that this meaning perspective is most often expressed as not only a denial of bias toward students of color, but also consequent denial of accommodations in school or classroom structure and policy necessary to meet these students' particular (and often cross-cultural) needs. These findings indicate that educators' own (often similar) biographies tend to foster a shared illusion of homogeneity with respect to what policy and structural emphases are appropriate for students of color. These influences and cultural filters, in turn, tend to prompt the denial of culturally sensitive school and classroom accommodations for the appropriate education of these students.

The second of these meaning perspectives noted among public school educators is most often associated with educators' perceptions of, and approaches toward, their Mexican American students. This meaning perspective is best described as the ideology of the "mañana conflict." The term "mañana," the Spanish word for "tomorrow," is descriptive of educators' shared, but contradictory, interpretation that Mexican American students hold no vision of a better tomorrow for themselves, and prefer to put off until tomorrow what they could be doing today. The term "conflict," in this case, is indicative of educators' battlefield perception of the educative relationship between teachers and their Mexican American students. Accordingly, the meaning perspective of the mañana conflict argues that Mexican American students vacillate about their education, are lazy, and are disinterested in learning and education, as are their parents. Ultimately, this meaning perspective further asserts that Mexican American students' (and their parents') attitudes toward education and schooling fosters a battlefield environment in which the education of these students is merely a chore that public school educators must endure.

This line of research does much to suggest that racial hatred in the public schools is not just phenomena of the distant past. It highlights the need for in-depth, ethnographic investigations of the deeply ingrained, and sometimes racist, attitudes of public school educators toward their students of color. Most important, these recent studies suggest that today's public school educators have been inadequately prepared for diversity in the school, especially preparation that would prompt critical reflection.

Sociopolitical perspective
{1980-Present}:
- •1980-1983—The tone for this era in race relations is set when President Reagan fails to back a bill to make Martin Luther King's birthday a national holiday.

- **1981**—The U.S. Civil Rights Commission [CRC] issues a report critical of Reagan's civil rights policies. In response, he becomes the first president to try packing the CRC with members sympathetic to his views. By 1982, he has succeeded in creating a conservative majority on the CRC Board.
- **1984-1988**—The U.S. Supreme Court, in *Grove City College v. Bell* (1984), markedly curtails the enforcement power of the Office of Civil Rights in higher education by ruling that if a college program practices discrimination, only that program can be deprived of federal funds, not all of the college's programs. Although the decision is later superseded by the Civil Rights Restoration Act (1988), serious racial imbalances at U.S. college campuses will remain the norm for the 1990s.
- **1988-1991**—Shortly before President George Bush signs the Civil Rights Act of 1991 (which he had vetoed in 1990), a memo written by White House Counsel C. Boyden Gray becomes public. The memo proposes the elimination of all government affirmative action programs and regulations adopted since the 1960s.
- **1992-1995**—Two key cases in the U.S. Supreme Court severely weaken the efforts of civil rights advocates to achieve school integration: *Freeman v. Pitts* (1992) and *Missouri v. Jenkins* (1995). The former case makes it easier for segregated school districts to escape federal court supervision and return to local control before desegregation has been achieved. The latter case undermines state funding of magnet schools as a means to school integration.
- **1993**—The Religious Freedom Restoration Act restores the standards of review for the American Indian Religious Freedom Act that were overturned by a Supreme Court Ruling in 1990.
- **1995**—To date, 22 states have passed English-only legislation on the grounds that bilingual education encourages ethnic tribalism and the breakdown of a cohesive society (Niemonen, 1997). Although a federal judge has struck down Arizona's official English law in 1990 on the grounds that it violates First Amendment Rights, a   1995 poll reveals that 73 percent of Americans and 33 percent of the members of Congress think that English should be the official language (Hedden, 1995).
- **1995-1996**—The Commission on Immigration Reform recommends the gradual reduction of legal immigration into the United States by at least one-third and the elimination of long-standing visa preferences for siblings and adult children (Pear, 1995). This recommendation ignores results of a recent cost benefit analysis conducted by Passel (1994). His research studied immigration from 1970-1992 and found that immigrants entering the United States during these years generated a surplus to the U.S. economy, conservatively estimated at between $25 billion and $35 billion.

Sociocultural perspective
{1980-Present}:
- **1983**—Approximately 46 percent of all U.S. citizens sentenced to prison are African American, despite the fact that African Americans constitute only 12 percent of the population (Rich, 1986).

- **1986**—While 50 to 80 percent of all inner-city students drop out of high school, one million teenagers cannot read above the 3rd-grade level, 28 percent of all students fail to receive high school diplomas, 50 percent of all college students drop out in their first year, and 33 percent of all adults are described as functionally or marginally illiterate (Bastian, Fruchter, Gittell, Greer, & Hoskins, 1986).
- **1994**—As the turn of the century approaches, Marian Wright Edelman (1994), President of the Children's Defense Fund, pauses to reflect upon the success of retrenchment vis-à-vis the state of children in America:

  Every sixteen seconds of every school day, as we talk about a competitive workforce in the future, one of our children drops out of school. Every 26 seconds, an American child runs away from home. These are not just poor or Black children—they are all of our children. . . . Every 47 seconds, a youngster is abused. Every 67 seconds a teenager has a baby. . . . Every seven minutes a child is arrested for a drug offense. . . . Every 53 minutes, in the richest land on earth, an American child dies of poverty. (p. 7)

  For Edelman, the standard of success in America is more focused on personal greed than on the common good. She argues that too many children of all races are growing up unable to handle life, and are uncertain and fearful about the future.
- **1994**—Richard Herrnstein and Charles Murray set off a firestorm of controversy with the publication of their book *The Bell Curve*. These authors reject the role of environment and culture in creating dependence and crime. Instead, they argue that intelligence is the best single explanation of social status, wealth, and poverty. They further contend that social pathologies such as poverty, illegitimacy, and welfare dependence are strongly related to low IQ. Most controversial is their argument that Blacks as a group are intellectually inferior to Whites. Critics immediately attack the book for its fallacious use of data to fit its political argument, as well as what have been interpreted as fundamental flaws in methodology and analytical techniques (Willie & Taylor, 1995).
- **1995**—Stephen Steinberg's book *Turning Black* attacks the emergence of a color-blind society as a "spurious justification for maintaining the racial status quo" (p. 15).
- **1997**—In an in-depth interview with *USA Today*'s editorial board ("A Retreat," 1997), Jesse Jackson, longtime civil rights advocate and leader, asserts that at least five factors evident in the 1990s indicate a major reversal of the gains made toward equity and civil rights: 1) an anti-immigrant/anti-minority backlash, evident in tougher immigration statutes, heightened searches of individuals, and nationwide polls that reflect a marked unwillingness among Americans to welcome new immigrants; 2) affirmative action statutes such as California's Proposition 209, which have already affected minorities' enrollment in U.S. colleges; 3) government downsizing, which, Jackson argues, adversely affects the African American middle class; 4) an alleged increase in the export of jobs since 1993 and the advent of legislation such as NAFTA; and 5) so-called welfare reform that, according to Jackson, has not only removed the safety net for many minorities, but also has adversely affected the Black middle class, many of whom are social workers. According to the editorial board of *USA Today*

(1997), the Urban Institute estimates that the 1996 welfare legislation will push 2.6 million people into poverty, including 1.1 million children.

Sociohistorical and racial violence perspective {1980-Present}:

- •1982—Detroit, Michigan: A Chinese American, Vincent Chin, is beaten to death by a White father and son who reportedly mistook him for being Japanese. The duo blame the Japanese for the loss of U.S. jobs. The father and son are sentenced to just three years' probation and fined $3,000 each. A later trial on federal civil rights charges ends in acquittal.
- •1986—Kansas City, Missouri: Carl Rosendahl fires shots into an African American family's home in a personal campaign to rid the neighborhood of the family. The incident is repeated two more times. After exploding a bomb in the family's back yard, Rosendahl finally is jailed.
- •1986—Howard Beach, New York: Three African Americans are attacked and beaten by a gang of Whites. Michael Griffith, one of the victims, is then struck and killed by a vehicle while trying to flee. Less than a year later, three White youths are convicted—of manslaughter, not murder—and a fourth is acquitted.
- •1989—Long Beach, California: Video cameras document the public beating of Don Jackson, an off-duty, African American police officer, by White patrolmen.
- •1991—Los Angeles, California: A man trying out a new video camera records the beating of Rodney King (an African American police suspect) by White patrolmen. King suffers multiple injuries, including broken ribs and severe damage to his left eye.
- •1992—Los Angeles, California: Police charged in the beating of Rodney King are acquitted by a jury that includes no African Americans. The verdict ignites widespread rioting, which results in 38 dead, 4,000 arrests, 3,700 buildings in ruin, and millions of dollars in property damage.
- •1997—The public reaction O. J. Simpson's acquittal on murder charges offers a unique and prototypical illustration of the increasing racial divide that is seldom comprehended by Whites; it also is indicative of the tremendous divergence of perception and opinion among Blacks and Whites. Although 83 to 87 percent of African Americans believe that justice was served, 78 to 86 percent of Whites believe that justice was denied because defense attorneys chose to play the "race card" to gain an acquittal grounded in emotions, rather than using reason (Niemonen, 1997).

RAGE

Rage is defined as madness, violent and uncontrolled anger; a fit of violent wrath; insanity; violent action; and a burning desire or passion (Webster, 1974, 1984). One must realize that racism has produced rage in both the abused and the abuser. It is an illness, albeit a psychological one, that has plagued society as we know it from its inception. How else can we explain the motivation for the genocidal treatment of Native Americans as described elsewhere in this chapter? How else can one explain the treatment of Native Americans, as discussed in Dee Brown's *Bury My Heart at Wounded Knee* (1970); the Mid-Atlantic Passage of the 18th and 19th centuries, when

millions of Black Africans perished under the most inhumane conditions while crossing the Atlantic Ocean to the United States; or the destruction of millions of Jews by
Germans while the rest of the world stood in silence? How do we explain the internment of thousands of American citizens of Japanese descent? The authors of this
chapter, as well as other writers (Grier & Cobbs, 1968; West, 1993), can only believe
that motivation for the aforementioned despicable human actions came from a rage
that had been cultivated in a social environment of racism.

The notion of racism ultimately resulting in rage, especially in the abused, was most
eloquently presented by two Black psychiatrists, William Grier and Price Cobbs,
during the late '60s and early '70s. One of the authors of this chapter had the privilege of hearing Dr. Cobbs describe a number of cases that illustrated the internal rage
manifested in many of his Black clients. Following are some quotations from their
bestseller *Black Rage* (Grier & Cobbs, 1968):

John's milieu from cradle to consultation room had put a penalty on success. He was allowed to
be outstanding among black people but was penalized when he competed successfully against
whites. This was consistent with his experience as a child. His parents were accepting of his
achievements as an obedient child, but they were critical of any advance beyond childhood. The
environment of his adult life was then perceived as reinforcing an unfortunate aspect of his
family experience. He was encouraged to be an outstanding "child Negro" but harsh penalties
were invoked if he behaved as an adult. This powerful interlocking of family milieu and social
attitudes has presented a barrier to him and his black brethren which is felt by no other ethnic
group in America.

One of the problems in understanding the discontent of black people in America is highlighted
in this material. The relationship between intrapsychic functioning and the larger social environment is exceedingly complex. Among other things, Negroes want to change inside but find it
more difficult to do so unless things outside are changed as well. It is clear that the simplistic
solution of "more education" is meaningless when a society is more attuned to race than it is to
academic achievement. (p. 21-22)

An abuser's rage was described as follows:

. . . Although she lived in a large area of expensive homes and although her own home cost
$150,000, she said she was most afraid of black people taking over her neighborhood.

The outrageously irrational quality of racial prejudice is evident in many aspects of the phenomenon. Housing bias is an example of a more far-reaching and influential effect. White people
have a deep and abiding feeling that the races are supposed to be separated and that the prefer-
ential places should be reserved for themselves.

To live near blacks or to eat with blacks is to jeopardize one's status. White people are supposed to eat and live in better places than black people.

The following example may help to illustrate how central is the attitude of white superiority in
this country.

The value of a home has come to be determined neither by the quality of the structure nor by
the value of the structures around it. It can be sharply devalued by the proximity of a family of
blacks. It is devalued because few other white families would purchase it, and unless it is sought

by other black families, the owner finds its market value very low indeed.

We know of no other ethnic group which by its mere proximity can so certainly make a man's home repugnant to him.

The wealthy woman in the example above was so troubled by the prospect of blacks moving into her neighborhood that she took a passionate stand for restrictive legislation in the hope of barring them more effectively. (Grier & Cobbs, 1968, p. 188)

One of the Black authors of this chapter is experiencing this same kind of housing racism in 1998. He and his wife are attempting to sell a house in a predominantly White neighborhood. He was advised by a White realtor to remove his family photographs from the home. The White realtor observed several White potential buyers reacting unfavorably after seeing the owners' family photographs on the mantle. The owners are an interracial couple. The husband of one White couple, after noticing a family photo, said to his wife, "Let's get out of here." Most professional Black couples have as much difficulty in selling as they do buying a home in a White neighborhood. They have learned through the grapevine that the following steps must be taken in this society if they are to be successful in selling their home:

- List with a White realtor.
- Remove all photographs and other items that would indicate that a Black family or interracial family resides there.
- Do not be present when the home is being shown.

Living in a racist society produces a certain paranoia that invades the psyche of even professional people of color. A Black professional was conversing with a younger man about a new project. He answered several questions about the proposal, some parts of which involved confrontation with White professionals. The older man was held in high esteem by Black people in the community. He had a distinguished record of service on community-wide committees and boards. To an outsider, he was as comfortable at a cocktail party as in his office. His professional activities were wide and multiracial. By almost any measure he would be regarded as successful.

As the exchange continued, the older man raised an objection to each question. He warned against angering "them." "They" might not like it; "they" would have thought of it first; "they" would have a different and therefore better proposal. He got angrier as the discussion continued. "They" became increasingly synonymous with all White people. He finally became exasperated and ended the conversation by saying, "Don't you know Charlie never sleeps?" (Grier & Cobbs, 1968, pp. 192-193).

The late Reginald Lewis recounts in his autobiography that one of his earliest childhood memories was hearing his grandparents tell about employment discrimination against African Americans. When asked for his opinion on the subject, 6-year-old Reginald simply replied: "Why should White guys have all the fun?" (Lewis & Walker, 1993). Lewis strongly felt that he had to be twice as good as Whites, and he drove those around him to give more than 100 percent.

In the area of sexual congress between races, prejudice reaches truly heroic heights of idiocy.

The culture seems to require that white people react with horror and revulsion to the idea of the sexual act occurring between whites and blacks. But the following incident is not unusual.

"A white girl told her mother that she had become engaged to a Negro. The mother fainted. On recovering, she asked: 'What color is he?' Next she asked: 'Does he have money?' And finally: 'What does he do?'"

Her questions indicate that she was so shocked by her daughter's engagement to a black that she had to search for some way to avoid its being known (if he were fair) or some way for it not to matter (if he were very rich) or some way to neutralize the effect partially (if he had a powerful position). She sounds very knowledgeable about the culture. She knows that, although everyone will react with shock to the news, people will really care less if the man is not a readily recognizable black. And even that will matter less if he is rich enough or powerful enough. (Grier & Cobbs, 1968, p. 189)

As Barbara Sizemore (1969) and others have pointed out, the true values of this racist society are maleness, White European ancestry, and money. Put these three values together and they equal power. The mother's reaction to her White daughter being engaged to a Black man is couched in the true values of our society.

Malcolm Little, better known as Malcolm X, perhaps embodies the rage of racism like no one else has before or since. As West wrote,

Malcolm X articulated black rage in a manner unprecedented in American history. His style of communicating this rage bespoke a boiling urgency and an audacious sincerity. The substance of what he said highlighted the chronic refusal of most Americans to acknowledge the sheer absurdity that confronts human beings of African descent in this country—the incessant assaults on black intelligence, beauty, character, and possibility. His profound commitment to affirm black humanity at any cost and his tremendous courage to accent the hypocrisy of American society made Malcolm X the prophet of black rage—then and now. (West, 1993, p. 95)

Malcolm X did, however, evolve out of his rage as very few people ever do:

. . . He was saved by a religious sect given to a strange, unhistorical explanation of the origin of black people and even stranger solutions to their problems. He rose to power in that group and outgrew it. Feeding on his own strength, growing in response to his own commands, limited by no creed, he became a citizen of the world and an advocate of all oppressed people no matter their color or belief. Anticipating his death by an assassin, he dis

In the area of sexual congress between races, prejudice reaches truly heroic heights of idiocy.

tilled, in a book, the essence of his genius, his life. His autobiography thus is a legacy and, together with his speeches, illustrates the thrusting growth of the man—his evolution, rapid, propulsive, toward the man he might have been had he lived.

The essence of Malcolm X was growth, change, and a seeking after truth.

Alarmed white people saw him first as an eccentric and later as a dangerous radical—a revolutionary without troops who threatened to stir black people to riot and civil disobedience. Publicly, they treated him as a joke; privately, they were afraid of him.

After his death he was recognized by black people as the "black shining prince" and recordings of his speeches became treasured things. His autobiography was studied, his life marveled at. Out of this belated admiration came the philosophical basis for black activism and indeed the thrust of Black Power itself, away from integration and civil rights and into the "black bag."

Unlike Malcolm, however, the philosophical underpinnings of the new black militancy were static. They remained encased within the ideas of revolution and black nationhood, ideas Malcolm had outgrown by the time of his death. His stature has made even his earliest statements gospel and men now find themselves willing to die for words which in retrospect are only milestones in the growth of a fantastic man.

Many black men who today preach blackness seem headed blindly toward self-destruction, uncritical of anything "black" and damning the white man for diabolical wickedness. For a philosophical base they have turned to the words of Malcolm's youth.

This perversion of Malcolm's intellectual position will not, we submit, be held against him by history.

Malcolm's meaning for us lies in his fearless demand for truth and his evolution from a petty criminal to an international statesman—accomplished by a black man against odds of terrible magnitude—in America. His message was his life, not his words, and Malcolm knew it. (Grier & Cobbs, 1968, pp. 201-202)

DIALOGUE, ENGAGEMENT, AND HEALING RACISM

In Harlon L. Dalton's book *Racial Healing: Confronting the Fear Between Blacks and Whites* (1995), he offers the following:

Engagement is critical to healing. It has the potential to transform our lives. It can change the way we see, hear, think, and feel. It can propel us across vast differences in culture and experience. It can move us past our fears. When we engage, truly engage, we let go and grab on at the same time. We lose our hold on old truths even as we reach out for new ones. We sacrifice neatness for the messiness of reality and comfort for the occasional pain of honest dealing. (p. 27)

Dalton's position, in our judgment, is essential and critical to our understanding of the healing process. Because of the feelings that have been generated by such engagement and dialogue, there have been times when neither the popular press nor the academic press would devote much space and energy to discussions about race. Ignoring the reality of racist practices and their impact on all of us has allowed it to become worse. Therefore, we see new evidence of racist thinking and behavior among very young Americans. Such thinking and behavior has created a climate of violence, urgency, and criminal activity. "As long as one refuses to acknowledge an illness or infirmity, one cannot expect any healing to begin" (James B. Boyer, personal communication).

We recognize that healing approaches require great courage and perception, because healing is a necessary ingredient to America's future. Dalton vividly describes the need for a changed mentality:

... at this particular moment in American history, meaningful action at the societal level is virtually impossible. As a nation we lack a consensus concerning how to deal with the problems that bedevil us most. We seem unable to take sustained action in any direction for very long. And we don't trust anyone enough to let them lead. We are, in short, politically paralyzed. (pp. 27-28)

While we recognize that Dalton's position sounds bleak, we must recognize that acknowledging the dilemma is the beginning of the healing process. It is important to recognize that Dalton is attempting to help us understand our own behavior on both sides of the "engagement" table so that we can proceed together toward some societal healing. All of this presupposes that most Americans actually want healing. Fear is not a useful emotion. Hate is certainly a destructive emotion.

What are some of the mistaken perceptions ingrained in society? Dalton (1995) indicates the following:

In the popular imagination, criminals are Black or Brown; crime victims White. Welfare cheats are dark of hue, the "forgotten middle class" is light. Governmental "taxing and spending" favors racial minorities and comes out of the hides of the White majority. Problem immigrants have yellow or brown skin; the citizens who foot the bill do not. (p. 28)

The author goes on to clarify that those are not his beliefs, but rather that the thinking about the nation's most pressing problems have become "racialized," which leads to fears about race.

When Martin Luther King, Jr., began to be so forceful about the outcomes of civil rights efforts and the healing of tension and fears generated by racism, he offered the following: "If you think I came to tell you to hate White people, you have the wrong man. Our goal is not to defeat or humiliate the White man, but to win his friendship and love" (*Jet Magazine*, April, 1968, p. 34). Although King was known for his non-violent philosophy, such dialogue was so powerful that persons unable to engage at that level often resorted to violent confrontation.

Our discussion of racism in the United States does not in any way imply a reflection or dislike of this country. Instead, our quest is for a healing of a relationship. As part of the healing, we may experience, on occasion, something like a lover's quarrel—but there is also devotion to the United States and the freedoms expressed in the great documents like the Constitution and the Bill of Rights. There is no point at which we deny the possibilities of a nation so great. It is only that our history is loaded with inhumane practices growing out of a racist mentality. We must fight the cultural misinformation that grew out of inappropriate practices.

Racism and Cultural Misinformation

In any oppressive situation or arrangement, especially one built on racist thinking and behavior, misinformation becomes a major roadblock to positive human relations.

Racism is the parent of discrimination. On the basis of racist thinking, discriminatory practices evolved, which, in turn, yielded cultural misinformation. If I believe that others are basically inferior to me, then I create thought patterns that reinforce this thinking. Furthermore, I will seek and digest information that supports such cultural frameworks. This is the type of thinking that has been so prevalent in the United States.

Historically, the separation of the races has resulted in powerful blocks of misinformation. Farai Chideya addressed this in her book *Don't Believe the Hype: Fighting Cultural Misinformation About African Americans* (1995). She reports the following in her book:

Q: Hasn't racism all but disappeared from today's society?
A: A 1990 study by the University of Chicago's National Opinion Research Center found that the majority of Whites still believe Blacks to be inferior. Among the results: 53% of non-Black respondents said they thought Blacks were less intelligent than Whites, 51% agreed Blacks were less patriotic, 62% thought Blacks were lazier, and 78% said that Blacks prefer to live off welfare. To a lesser degree, Hispanics and southern Whites were pegged with the same stereotypes. (pp. 183-184)

Given this kind of data, we now must revisit the source of such beliefs and how they affect thinking about policy, program, and procedure in society's institutions. If this chasm still exists, then members of Congress, educators, politicians at the local and state levels, and members of corporate boards and school boards, as well as scores of others who make policies, must engage the issue at a very serious level if the healing is to begin.

While this may sound like all the healing effort must originate with those who have benefited most—meaning White Americans—that is not the case. African Americans, Hispanics and/or Latinos, Native Americans, and others who have factors in such equations have a responsibility to examine their own emotional baggage. At the same time, one must constantly re-examine the setting in which the engagement is to occur. Lani Guinier offers the following: "In a racially divided society, majority rule may become majority tyranny" (cited in Bell, 1986).

What About Friendships Across Racial Lines?
Chideya (1995) reports that since many young people today have friends of other races, they assume that such friendships eradicate the institutional racism. Again citing the Chicago study, she posits:

Over 70% of all youths said they have at least one good friend of another race. But like the halfhearted social apology, "Oh, I have a friend who's black," friendships do not eliminate underlying bias. States the report, "Personal friendships may contribute to better understanding but do not bridge the gap between groups created by stereotypes or myths. Young White focus group participants told moving stories about friendships with individual Blacks, while repeating or assenting to negative cliches pinned on Blacks as a group, such as 'lazy' or 'waiting for a handout.' " (pp. 184-185)

Despite these friendships, society will never be free of racism until institutional practices are changed. Misinformation is one of the most complex detriments to the elimination of racist thought and behavior.

The Problem of White Superiority

The historical perceptions of White superiority are so powerful that one cannot study United States history without recognizing the absence of diversity in a country that supposedly welcomes all. This land of the free and home of the brave has had human relations problems since its beginning. We are now addressing this hypocrisy.

In a system that teaches and demonstrates White Superiority, many persons of color embrace that myth. As noted Black nationalist Marcus Garvey said to his Black colleagues in 1923: "Every man has a right to his own opinion. Every race has a right to its own action; therefore, let no man persuade you against your will, let no other race influence you against your own" (cited in Bell, 1986).

The Stigma of Black Inferiority

William M. Banks (1996) indicates that of all the ideological roadblocks to equality, the belief that Blacks were mentally inferior to persons of other races was the most challenging. We must, however, discuss the varying perceptions historically associated with this belief. For example, Thomas Jefferson (a slave owner) acknowledged Blacks to be equal to Whites in terms of bravery, tolerance for heat, and emotionality, but considered them "inferior to Whites in the endowments of body and mind" (Banks, 1996, pp. 31-32).

Benjamin Banneker, the noted Black scientist-surveyor and mathematician, in challenging Thomas Jefferson's assertion, experienced confusion when his intellectual prowess was dismissed by influential Whites. Banks (1996) relates the following:

Black thinkers identified with Banneker's scientific contribution, believing it vindicated their own claims to intellectual stature and potential. Surely the achievements of a self-taught free Black gave evidence of the potential repressed by slavery. Yet, individual samples of merit, however numerous, failed to shake the beliefs of a racist culture. Like Jefferson, skeptics disingenuously claimed fraud, charging that the alleged achievements of Blacks were in fact the work of White accomplices. Others attributed the talent of Blacks to the flow of "white blood" in their veins. (p. 32)

It is our belief that dialogue (as a constant instructional and procedural entity) will be essential to healing this kind of chasm. Furthermore, it is critical that those participating in the healing process become aware of the powerful role that dialogue, engagement, and optimism play in healing a nation. Racial healing cannot occur unless participating parties understand that such healing is a collaborative process. As Martin Luther King, Jr., said, "We must live together as brothers, or perish together as fools" (*Jet Magazine*, April, 1968, p. 34).

Dalton (1995) suggests that the challenge for White Americans is to realize, even when they are not in the minority, that their race matters, too. It establishes their place in the social pecking order. It hangs over the relationships they establish with people of color. Like it or not, their unchosen racial identity has a profound influence on their lives.

References

Banks, W. M. (1996). *Black intellectuals: Race and responsibility in American life.* New York: W. W. Norton & Company.

Bastian, A., Fruchter, N., Gittell, M., Greer, C., & Hoskins, K. (1986). *Choosing equality.* Philadelphia, PA: Temple University.

Bell, J. C. (1986). *Famous black quotations.* New York: Warner Books.

Blumer, H. (1958). Race prejudice as a sense of group position. *Pacific Sociological Review, 1,* 3-7.

Brown, D. (1970). *Bury my heart at Wounded Knee: An Indian history of the American West.* New York: Holt, Rinehart.

Summary

This discourse does not attempt to provide a chronological history of racist characteristics, behaviors, laws, policies, or practices. Instead, it attempts to select certain realities to help us understand, historically, how we emerged with the current thinking about our lives, institutions, careers, families, friends, and neighborhoods. While all agencies must be engaged in the healing process, the American school—because it touches the lives of almost every citizen—has a pivotal role to play in influencing thinking. Therefore, those involved with program or curriculum design, teacher education, staff development, program planning, testing and evaluation, and all other aspects of school must open themselves up to serious dialogue.

Dialogue that assumes that one race is superior to another breeds mistrust, misuse of power, and the perpetuation of misinformation. Healing will only begin when people of dif-ferent races meet as social equals, with all that that implies, to begin a dialogue. Broadening our understanding of each other is vital. Since schools assume responsibility as the guardians of knowledge, then we suggest that they become leaders in this healing attempt.

Chideya, F. (1995). Don't believe the hype: Fighting cultural misinformation about African Americans. New York: Penguin.

Dalton, H. L. (1995). Racial healing: Confronting the fear between Blacks and Whites. New York: Doubleday.

Daniels, R. (1988). Asian America: Chinese and Japanese in the United States since 1850. Seattle, WA: University of Washington.

Edelman, M. W. (1994). Investing in our children: A struggle for America's conscience and future. In F. Schultz (Ed.), Multicultural education: 94/95 (pp. 6-9). Guilford, CT: Dushkin Publishing Group.

Grier, W., & Cobbs, P.M. (1968). Black rage. New York: Basic Books.

Grobsmith, E. S., & Ritter, B. R. (1992). The process of restoration of a federally terminated tribe. Human Organization, 51, 2.

Hedden, S. (1995, September 25). One nation, one language? U.S. News & World Report, 38-42.

Hernstein, R. J., & Murray, C. (1996). The bell curve: Intelligence and class structure in American life. New York: Free Press.

Herrera, S. (1996). Junior high school teachers and the meaning perspectives they hold regarding their Mexican American students: An ethnographic case study. Dissertation Abstracts International, 56(12), 4643. (CD-ROM). Abstract From: ProQuest File: Dissertation Abstracts Item: AAC 9610795.

Jatras, J. G. (1997). Benevolent global hegemony. Chronicles, 21(6), 26-38.

Kivel, P. (1996). Uprooting racism: How white people can work for racial justice. Philadelphia, PA: New Society Publishers.

LeVine, M. L. (1996). African Americans and civil rights: From 1619 to the present. Phoenix, AZ: Oryx.

Lewis, R., & Walker, B. (1993). Why should white guys have all the fun? New York: John Riley and Sons.

McLemore, S. D., & Romo, R. (1985). The origins and development of the Mexican American people. In R. O. De La Garza, F. D. Bean, C. M. Bonjean, R. Romo, & R. Alvarez (Eds.), The Mexican American experience: An interdisciplinary anthology (pp. 33-56). Austin, TX: University of Texas.

Mezirow, J. (1991). Transformative dimensions of adult learning. San Francisco, CA: Jossey-Bass.

Murry, K. (1996). Reflective-transformative professional development predicated upon critical reflection and enabled by a school-university partnership: A microethnographic case study. Dissertation Abstracts International, 56(08), 3075. (CD-ROM). Abstract From: ProQuest File: Dissertation Abstracts Item: AAC 9541766.

Newsmakers. (1968, April). Jet Magazine, 34.

Niemonen, J. (1997). The race relations problematic in American sociology: A case study and critique. American Sociologist, 28(1), 15-26.

Passel, J. (1994). A reappraisal of Huddle's "The cost of immigrants." PRIP-UI-29. Washington, DC: Urban Institute.

Pear, R. (1995, June). Change of policy on U.S. immigrants is urged by panel. New York Times, 5, p. A1.

Retreat of civil rights, A. (1997, May 12). USA Today, pp. A2-A9.

Rich, S. (1986, February). Blacks on the bottom: For an underclass of the poor and alienated, life is only getting worse. The Washington Post National Weekend Edition, 10, p. 3.

Rostow, E. V. (1945, September). Our worst wartime mistake. Harper's Magazine, pp. 193-201.

Schermerhorn, R. (1970). Comparative ethnic relations: A framework for theory and research. New York: Random House.

Shakeshaft, C. (1986). A gender at risk. Phi Delta Kappan, 67(7), 496-506.

Sizemore, B. (1969). Separation: A reality approach to inclusion? In R. L. Green (Ed.), Racial crisis in American education (pp. 249-279). Chicago: Pollett Educational Corp.

Steinberg, S. (1995). Turning black. Boston: Beacon.

Webster's New Collegiate Dictionary. (1974). Springfield, IL: G&C Merriam Co.

Webster's II New Riverside University Dictionary. (1984). Boston: Houghton Mifflin.

West, C. (1993). Race matters. Boston: Beacon Press.

Willie, C., & Taylor, H. (1995, March). The bell curve debate. Paper presented at the Annual Meeting of the Eastern Sociological Society, Philadelphia, Pennsylvania.

Wilson, W. J. (1973). Race, power, and privilege: Race relations in theoretical and sociohistorical perspectives. New York: The Free Press.

Section 2

instructional perspectives

chapter III

Healing the Wounds of Instructional Racism

Patricia J. Larke, *Texas A&M University*
Gwendolyn Webb-Johnson, *University of Texas at Austin*
Ronald Rochon, *University of Wisconsin - La Crosse*
Mary Anderson, *City University of New York*

Historically, instruction within U.S. schools has perpetuated the values and culture of Western ideology, regardless of the students' cultural diversity. Racism has affected the classroom's academic and social interactions. As learning environments become more culturally diverse, the necessity for instruction to respond to the learner's culture becomes critical. Unfortunately for students whose cultural orientations differ from Eurocentric perspectives, critical components of their learning process often are negated; thus, their academic performance may not be an accurate assessment of their ability. In large measure, the information selected by teachers, and how they teach it, is still based on a Eurocentric cultural orientation. Consequently, the impact of racism in instruction must be examined to help ensure the academic success of students of color, and for poor children. The purpose of this chapter, then, is to provide 1) a definition of instructional racism, 2) an overview of the construct and its relationship to instructional strategy, and 3) strategies that may facilitate a change in instructional design.

Definition of Instructional Racism

At the heart of racism is the belief that one racial/ethnic group is superior to others and that racial equality does not exist. Racism often manifests itself, whether overtly or covertly, in the way that people and institutions think, act, and behave in society. According to the Office of Civil Rights, racism includes the attitudes, actions, or institutional structures that the dominant cultural group uses over minority cultural groups (Omi & Winant, 1994). One of the most recent definitions states that,

A simple understanding of racism is a set of beliefs about the superiority or inferiority of a group of people based on race. This set of beliefs can be ranked on the basis of inherited biological traits that produce unequal mental, personality, and cultural characteristics. However, because of the shifting of multiple meanings in race, and its embeddedness in power relations of the society, no simple definition of racism is sufficient. Wellman (1993) argues that racism is not merely prejudice or bigotry and should not be confused with ethnic hostilities, but rather it is "the culturally sanctioned beliefs which, regardless of the intentions involved, defend the advantages Whites have because of the subordinated position of racial minorities" (p. 4). Omi & Winant (1994) define racism "as fundamental characteristics or social projects which create or reproduce structures or dominations based on essentialist categories of race." (Grant & Ladson-Billings, 1997, p. 231)

Thus, within the United States and other geographical areas that historically were conquered and controlled by Western Europeans, racism continues to be associated with "white supremacy." Although many associate racism as a western construct, its tradition and roots were permeated in global communities centuries ago (Williams, 1987). For the purpose of this chapter, the authors examine racism from a curricular perspective as it influences instruction in U.S. classrooms. We propose that instructional racism often includes educators' "dysconscious" decisions. According to King (1991),

Dysconsciousness is an uncritical habit of mind (including perceptions, attitudes, assumptions and beliefs) that justifies inequality and exploitation by accepting the existing order of things as given. . . . [It] is a form of racism that tacitly accepts dominant White norms and privileges. It is not the absence of consciousness (that is, unconsciousness) but an impaired consciousness that distorts ways of thinking about race as compared to critical consciousness. (p. 133-134)

King states that this dysconsciousness can be applied to other forms of exploitation and is therefore undergirded in our definition of instructional racism. Within this critical consciousness is an uncritical way of thinking about racial inequality. It is related to the culturally sanctioned assumptions, beliefs, and myths that justify the social and economic advantages of a "privileged" group. The authors' interpretation of this conceptual framework of instructional racism is supported by research on the impact of institutional racism in society and schools (Banks & Banks, 1995; Grant, 1992; Takaki, 1993), and by King's research (1991) on dysconscious ideology. Several basic assumptions relate to the teaching process. One assumption is that teachers are committed to improving academic outcomes for "all" students. The effective teacher, however, must clearly differentiate between the intention and the impact of this assumption. The worthy premise of intent—a commitment to all students—often is clouded by the reality that many culturally diverse children experience less than optimal education outcomes in K-12 school settings in the United States. This belief system, by definition, promotes a "status quo concept of learning" and, by design, negates the need to provide *all* learners with the critical analytical skills to reconstruct learning environments based on equity in issues of power, privilege, and culture. While teachers may want to do an effective job, they often are perplexed by the reality that "best" theory and practice is ineffective with many children and youth of color. Figure 1 denotes several pathways leading to and from instructional racism.

Pathways To and From Instructional Racism

Figure 1

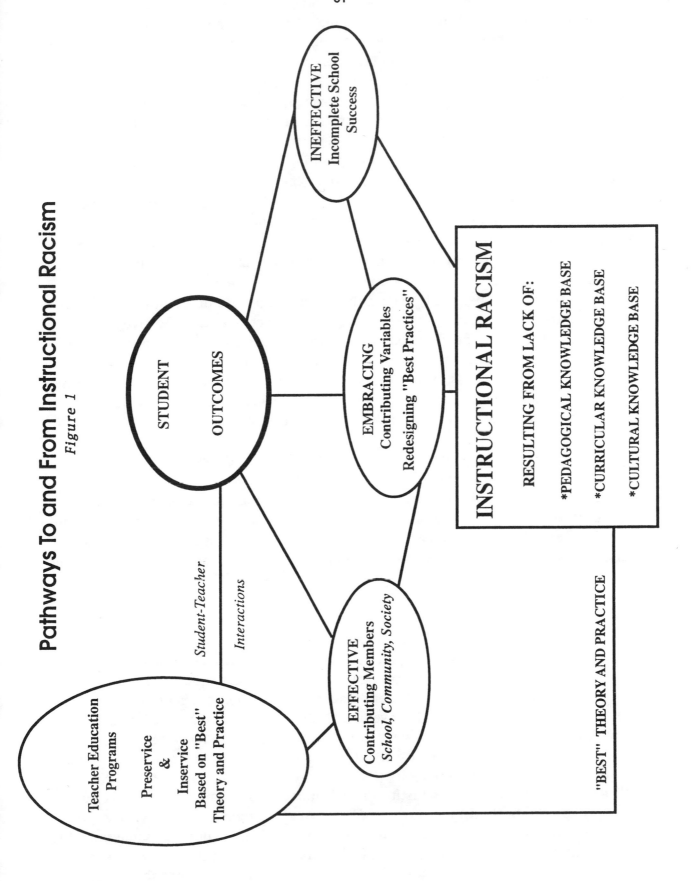

Instruction and curriculum are based on teacher preparation and development paradigms grounded in "best" theory and practice ideology. Student and teacher interactions often depend upon methods and procedures teachers learned during preservice and inservice programming. Effective classroom interactions will help prepare students to become productive members of schools, the community, and society. Sometimes, however, it is necessary to redesign certain tenets of "best" practice. If a student clearly demonstrates a physical or learning disability, for example, instructional practice can be modified to meet specific needs. Such an intervention may then lead to effective student outcomes. Unfortunately, many teaching interactions do not incorporate such contributing variables, and instructional practice and its impact can lead to instructional racism. Such instructional racism, then, may be manifested due to a lack of, or a limited knowledge base in, culturally responsive and curricularly sound pedagogical practice as it relates to embracing the integrity and academic strengths of all students.

Effective teachers consistently extend their knowledge base in culturally responsive pedagogy, and systematically assess the impact of effective and ineffective student outcomes. The authors purport that the majority of teachers who teach culturally diverse students lack the knowledge base to facilitate academic growth. As a result, *wanting* to do a good job is insufficient. Biased instructional behavior often will lead to predictable and inadequate student outcomes. Inconsistencies among belief systems further contribute to the pervasiveness of teachers' lowered expectations for students of color and for poor children. Instructional racism, then, is the impact of the relationships among biased unconscious, conscious, and dysconscious ideologies about instruction. These biased ideologies promote institutionalized beliefs of a particular cultural group over those of historically marginalized populations (i.e., African Americans, Asian Americans, Hispanic Americans, and Native Americans) and poor children. These children and youth often experience limited access to educational opportunities by virtue of the fact that their ethnicity, race, and socioeconomic status are perceived as deficits.

Overview of the Framework and Its Relationship to Instructional Strategy

As it does in elementary and secondary schools, instructional racism also manifests itself in higher education settings, particularly in teacher education programs at the preservice and inservice levels. Student-teacher interactions, curriculum (hidden or not), and policy are the traditional avenues through which instructional racism is maintained and sanctioned. The very content and nature of educating teachers to teach largely excludes the diversity of cultures, values, beliefs, and actions that many children bring with them to schools.

Within the United States, the institutional foundation of formal education is legitimized by the established social norms of Western philosophical ideology. The cyclical pattern of validating social thoughts and actions by virtue of those same thoughts and actions particularizes the nature and value of social interactions and expectations. This construct then defines and shapes what and how teachers should teach. When home and community socialization patterns match established social norms within schools, instructional practices often lead to predictable and desirable student outcomes for students whose behaviors best match those norms. Undesirable student outcomes are equally predictable when students' socialization patterns do not match established norms. Consequently, academic success has more to do with established institutional mandates than with individual student behaviors and needs.

Nevertheless, students of color and poor children often are blamed for academic failure. Teachers often believe that students of color and poor children are not capable of demonstrating educational excellence, because their degree of care, commitment, and persistence does not match teacher expectations (Delpit, 1988, 1995; Nieto, 1996). The failure is presumed to be inherent within the child. This practice is reinforced by what are known as "deficit theories" (Grossman, 1995). Data consistently shows that children of color and poor children receive lower grades, pass fewer classes, and are suspended in significantly greater proportions to their enrollment numbers when compared to European American learners (Harry & Anderson, 1994; U.S. Department of Education, 1995, 1996). As a result, teachers often use ineffective teaching strategies when students do not respond as expected. Teachers' lack of knowledge is often coupled with a reactive pedagogy that devalues the integrity of children of color and poor children. As a result, these children continue to perform poorly in school.

The impact of instructional racism manifests itself within the instructional delivery system in several ways. Students are compelled to be involuntary and, often, eventually willing participants in this construct (Delpit, 1995; Ladson-Billings, 1994; Woodson, 1933). These children and youth may demonstrate poor and/or ineffective instructional strengths in the classroom. They often resist academic engagement out of a fear or belief that failure is inevitable. They come to believe that academic excellence is a standard held by superior or uncontrollable forces that are out of their realm. Thus, educators who practice instructional racism essentially engineer such conclusions.

Instructional Racism in Classroom Contexts

The authors of this chapter presently are involved in a series of research studies examining the instructional interactions of teachers and students in general and special education settings. They hope to identify the interaction themes that will benefit culturally diverse students' academic performance. Through observations and teacher interviews, the following examples highlight what "instructional racism" looks like in the context of the classroom and school environment. The brief profiles of Youxi, Raul, Anatheia, Hasan, Shanequa, and Jamel—all students of color—demonstrate the occurrence and impact of instructional racism. It is noted that the teachers made pedagogical decisions that promised less than desirable academic outcomes for these youth. Such practices create scenarios that increase the likelihood of continued lowered expectations and dismal education outcomes for those who are already disproportionately represented in lower-level academic course work or tracks, special education classrooms, and suspension and expulsion rates (Artiles & Trent, 1994; Jones, 1989).

As mentioned previously, even though all of the students were expected to behave appropriately, teachers were more likely to modify their own behavior in a favorable way toward European American students who were demonstrating similar "inappropriate" responses. Excuses (like the ones in the following scenarios) were not made for European American students. In fact, few teachers even demonstrated negative attitudes about their European American students. They demonstrated lowered expectations for the academic success of students of color, and they routinely corrected the language used by African American and second-language acquisition students.

The following scenarios are some examples of what this construct looks like in the context of the classroom and school environment. The examples are excerpts taken from transcripts of observations conducted by the authors.

Youxi (Asian American female, age 10).

Youxi: (*Working on computation skills in multiplication.*) This stuff is hard. You know I cannot do it.

Teacher: I want you to try.

Youxi: I do not want to try. Just give me problems with my 1-5 tables; sixes and sevens are too hard. You make me do this cause I'm Asian. You think I'm smart in everything, but this hard.

Teacher: Honey, you should have said, "This is difficult," not, "This hard." I know you can do this. You are just not working hard enough. I am really surprised that you are complaining. Now you just concentrate. Your brother was such a good student.

Youxi's teacher does not acknowledge and affirm the fact that increased skill building in math challenges Youxi's threshold of comfort. She ignores the opportunity to demonstrate to Youxi how much of the times tables she in fact already knows, by virtue of the fact that she is proficient in the first five sets of tables. Rather than acknowledging and embracing Youxi's strengths, then confronting the skill deficits and taking on the responsibility to teach replacement behaviors designed to address the skill deficits, the teacher facilitates a false sense of academic worth.

The teacher's attempt to challenge Youxi ensures her continued academic failure, because she does not encourage Youxi to practice the needed skills. The teacher instead expects her to fulfill the role of the "model" student. Perhaps by operating on stereotypes about the academic ability of Asian students, the teacher ignores Youxi's individual needs. While the teacher feels compelled to acknowledge Youxi's frustration by telling her she is complaining, Youxi is experiencing instructional racism. She is made to feel "dumb." Making the decision that Youxi is not working hard enough devalues her efforts. Using the term "honey" is often perceived as condescending, which may also devalue the student.

Raul (Hispanic male, age 12).

Raul: I got a 42 on my vocabulary test. Man! (*mumbles in Spanish*)

Teacher: There is no "man" in this classroom. I know that you are disappointed in your grade, but we will work harder on the next test. I have told you repeatedly that you are not to speak Spanish in this class. Speak English. Now let's go on.

The teacher's comments indicate that mastery of concepts is not important. While Raul is promised the opportunity to try harder on the next test, he receives no replacement skills to help him negotiate his current academic challenges. Raul is made to feel inadequate. Speaking Spanish, his primary language, is not affirmed. He, too, is experiencing instructional racism. Such teacher behavior increases the likelihood that Raul would have negative school experiences; thus, limiting his choices of career opportunities.

Anatheia (Native American female, age 13).

Anatheia: I ain't doing homework, I ain't got time.

Teacher: Let's make a deal. If you promise to work really hard every day during class, you won't have any work to do at home. I know how hard it must be to live in those conditions on the reservation. I really want you to work on your use of "ain't." You know that is unacceptable language in my classroom. If you stop daydreaming so much during class you can get finished. I want you to be successful.

Anatheia complains about the work outside of class. Her teacher then feels compelled to make Anatheia a deal difficult to refuse. Students are made to feel "dumber" in their quest to avoid a challenge. The teacher demonstrates little understanding of spirituality as it relates to dimensions of Native American culture. She then makes assumptions about Anatheia's life on the reservation, and how she spends her class time. While work outside of class might create more challenges for some students than for others, do the alternatives have to include the exclusion of homework? If many students of color are already behind in expected academic skill development, are they likely to catch up without the benefit of systematic study that reaches beyond normal school hours? Anatheia is also the victim of instructional racism. The teacher lowers her expectations, believing that having Anatheia complete homework might interfere with her free time or her comfort level. Such a practice decreases the likelihood of Anatheia's academic success. Daily homework can indeed become her reality when she is encouraged and expected to make time for daily extensions beyond the classroom.

Hasan (African American male, age 13).

Teacher: (*Looking over her entire classroom.*) I am really disappointed in the way this science class behaved in my absence. You should be ashamed of yourselves. I am so disappointed. You know some of you can't afford to act out.

Hasan: (*Talks out.*) Why you looking at me? I didn't do nothing. I wasn't talking.

Teacher: You are talking now. I am looking at you because you are always talking.

Hasan: But I didn't do anything when the substitute was here. Ask him.

Teacher: You are talking now. You are lucky you have parents who take time to care, but you are always talking.

Hasan: Why you got to talk about my family? You always accusing me.

Teacher: You need to be quiet now, or you get a detention.
Hasan: I can't serve no detention. I have a football game.
Teacher: You just earned yourself 45 minutes.
Hasan: That's not fair.

Hasan takes very personally his teacher's charge of inappropriate behavior by the entire class in her absence. While she indeed begins by targeting the entire class, Hasan believes that he is unfairly included, making him uncomfortable. His "member to member" (Nichols, 1976) cultural orientations have socialized him to be keenly aware and responsive to social interactions highlighted by care and trust.

Understanding Hasan's cultural orientation is key to understanding how this scenario demonstrates instructional racism. While the teacher was talking to the entire class, Hasan felt singled out. He took the attack personally. His reaction could have been expected and, most important, avoided if the teacher understood the dynamics of social interactions often found among African American learners. While his talking out may not have been appropriate according to his teacher's expectations and guidelines, he did try to assure her that he did not do anything wrong in her absence. The teacher easily could have acknowledged his assertion and continued to confront the entire class. She chose, however, to engage in a conversation with Hasan that pushed each of them further and further into a struggle for control. Thus, instruction did not take place, and students were blamed for a substitute's inability to facilitate effective instruction. An attempt to appeal to the conscience of the entire class only succeeded in compelling Hasan to appeal for his innocence. Instructional racism was reinforced; the teacher felt compelled to blame, and Hasan felt compelled to defend. Who, then, is the instructional leader?

> The teacher felt compelled to blame, and Hasan felt compelled to defend. Who, then, is the instructional leader?

Shanequa (African American female, age 14).

Teacher: Please read the first page of the worksheet.
Shanequa: In 1492, Columbus sailed the ocean blue. But he didn't discover no America. (*Class laughs.*)
Teacher: I asked you to read the sheet. Would you like to continue?
Shanequa: Sure, but he might have sailed, but he didn't discover no America.
Teacher: That was improper use of the word "no." And, you just talked out. Your name goes in the book.
Shanequa: That's not fair. I was telling you this form is wrong.

Teacher: It is not your place to do anything but follow instructions.
Shanequa: DOG!!
Teacher: There are no dogs in this social studies classroom. You now have detention.

Shanequa responds honestly to another worksheet episode in her classroom, especially one that includes historically inaccurate information that some teachers persist in sharing. Shanequa was animated, demonstrating verve, oral tradition, and expressive individualism (Boykin, 1983), and she was persistent in her attempt to make a point. The curriculum offered did not present critical, accurate, or a holistic perception about Columbus's voyage. Shanequa's independent thinking was devalued, although she apparently possessed more accurate information than her teacher about the issue.

Jamel (African American male, age 10). While Jamel is in a general education 5th-grade classroom, he demonstrates early 1st-grade reading skills. He has participated in special education resource programs for the past four years. He received virtually no consistent instruction. When he was provided instruction, he was isolated from peers to complete worksheets. He did not learn the critical analytic skills that would help him reconstruct and negotiate the learning environment. A lack of belief in his ability, along with instruction limited to worksheets and coloring books, frames a very inappropriate pedagogical reality for Jamel. He is deeply entrenched in a setting dominated by instructional racism.

While Jamel did receive some resource services, the bulk of his day by mid-semester was spent sleeping on a classroom sofa. On several occasions throughout one month, Jamel was observed sleeping or coloring in a book after he returned from the resource room. On one occasion, when Jamel was allowed to work on the computer, the teacher withdrew this privilege because he cheered when the computer "cheered," noting his choice of a correct response. Jamel's response was to return to his sofa; within several minutes he was asleep.

While Jamel had few discipline problems his first two years in the new school environment, he had several problems in the 5th grade. He was caught taking a book from the bookmobile. He refused to follow instructions on several occasions during resource and general class time. He was reprimanded for making sexual references during lunch time. While these behaviors clearly were inappropriate, it did not help Jamel to label him a "developing criminal" or a "perpetrator of sexual harassment." He was embarrassed by public reprimands. Teacher responses to each of these situations were reactive and lacking in culturally responsive and effective practice, and seemed to reflect stereotypes about African American males as perpetuators of "sexual" and criminal behavior. Teachers and administrators made such comments as, "He is sexually harassing students," "He is well on his way to a life of crime," "That is such despicable behavior in a 10-year-old," "He needs to be staffed to a more restrictive setting," and "That's why the other students are frightened of him."

Jamel's case demonstrates further evidence of instructional racism. Teachers and other service providers consciously and dysconsciously provided systematic treatment predicated by reduced and sometimes nonexistent expectations of academic growth. The teacher (who admitted being frustrated) and the principal patiently awaited the completion of a formal assessment, hoping for a diagnosis of a significant cognitive disability or a behavioral disorder. Their plan was to recommend a more restrictive environment, because they had concluded that a setting for students demonstrating behavioral disorders would be more appropriate.

The authors understand that many practitioners might counter this argument by saying that the same scenario could be found with a poor European American student. It could. However, teachers' reactions to a 10-year-old European American who experiences educational deficits while also demonstrating socially inappropriate school behavior often are much different. In Jamel's situation, several European American boys in his classroom also were not working up to their academic potential. They made inappropriate comments with sexual overtones, as well. Those behaviors did not motivate the teacher to draw conclusions about the educational promise or future of those students. Their behaviors were considered developmental and worthy of "appropriate interventions" because they were "just little boys" experiencing some academic challenges or sexual explorations. Their behavior was considered worthy only of teachers making them aware that certain comments were inappropriate in the classroom context.

Jamel, on the other hand, was considered deviant. Teachers made assumptions about his home life, his parents, and his future based on a belief that he should be grateful to be in his particular school setting. They believed that he was making trouble and probably had no control over such behavior. It is also important to note here that when the words "instructional racism" were used to describe the teachers' behavior, they became angry and defensive. While the defense mechanism persisted, focus on Jamel's success and a consistent effort to share contextual information about him as an individual and about his cultural orientations eventually made a difference in their response, and, most important, in his improved academic and social skills standings. In this situation, the teachers had to change their belief system and their pedagogical actions. When they did, Jamel began to demonstrate improvement in his reading and in his social interactions.

This argument, however, goes beyond whether or not any given educational dilemma could happen to any learner. We believe that teachers' lowered expectations for students of color, and specifically in the case of Jamel, adversely affected pedagogical decisions. The teacher and principal drew conclusions about Jamel that deemed him unworthy of educational intervention. Because of biased assessment practices and subjective teacher judgment, these professionals concluded that he should be labeled as having a severe learning disability because he scored on the borderline for a "normal" IQ. The special education resource teacher was merely waiting for a re-evaluation because she was convinced that "[Jamel] is retarded." In fact, she asserted that until an assessment told her otherwise, she would treat him as retarded. Service providers did not believe that Jamel could learn. He was perceived as "strange" and in need of specialized service beyond the resource level. Little conversation or instructional planning addressed what he had learned, needed to learn, and, most important, wanted to learn.

Jamel was made to feel like a second-class citizen among his peers because no one in the school context deemed him worthy of any systematic instruction. He was made to feel less important. The teacher took on the mission of creating a "special environment" because of her inability to meet his unique needs, which were viewed as "deficits." He was the only African American student in his 5th-grade class. He was bused in from the "Black" side of town. His verve (i.e., propensity toward high levels of activity) was not embraced (Boykin, 1983). Often he was told to calm down and to stop fidgeting. The strengths he brought to the classroom were never assessed. The teacher expected him to behave and learn the same thing, in the same way, and at the same times as his same-aged peers. She gathered no data to address his academic skill strengths or deficits. With the support of her administrator, she patiently awaited a formal assessment that matched their conclusion, which was based on frustration.

While Jamel's example is extreme, it demonstrates the potential and real impact of instructional racism, as do the more subtle examples highlighted in the cases of Youxi, Raul, Anatheia, Hasan, and Shanequa. The implied and actual manifestations of racism systematically contribute to incomplete and devastating academic outcomes for many children of color and for poor children. While some educators' defensive counter-arguments are to be expected, the authors assert that such a response is a simple solution to an extremely complex construct. Teaching is rendered ineffective when educators fail to develop a knowledge base that values and respects the integrity of every child. If any of their pedagogical decisions are based on a lack of belief in student success because of their race or socio-economic status, those educators are participating in instructional racism. The outcomes are predictable. Such students will continue to experience failure. Often, these students are the only students of color in the classroom. Their teachers wanted them to behave "like the other children" and wondered why the student of color was the only student experiencing a problem. In Jamel's case, for example, teachers often asked why he was so verbal and angry all the time. When interviewed by an African American psychologist, Jamel explained that he was not angry, he was merely tired of people "picking" on him.

In each of the above scenarios, the authors observed and noted that each teacher desired to make a difference in the lives of their students. Unfortunately, the teachers lacked a knowledge base about the cultures of students of color, and they demonstrated little cultural and sociopolitical knowledge about instructional strategies that would assist them in their quest to make an educational difference. Effective instructional practices require a knowledge base, commitment, experience, and action in embracing the differences among children. While many of the above examples focused on African American learners, the scenarios are often similar for other children of color and for children of poverty (Payne, 1995).

Healing the Wounds:
Instructional Strategies

Healing the wounds of instructional racism requires, first and foremost, the recognition that racism does exist within the education system, and that such recognition is not the cry of a "blame the victim" syndrome. Research suggests that several "players" within the education system—including professors (specifically, teacher educators), elementary and secondary teachers, and administrators—can significantly decrease instructional racism. In addition, certain disciplines, policies, programs, and practices can be helpful as well. Multicultural instructional strategies, for example, are effective steps toward eradicating instructional racism.

The research on best practices for making curriculum changes to combat instructional racism supports the following:

- For instructional change to be effective, the desire for change must begin with the individual (Banks, 1994; Fullan, 1993; Grant, 1992; Grossman, 1995).
- Principles of effective instruction recognize that racism, bias, and discrimination exist in curriculum, in teaching, and in educational institutions, and how one responds to the existence is critical to their continuation or elimination (Adams & Welsch, 1995; Garcia, 1994; Kierstead & Wagner, 1993; Swartz, 1992).
- Teachers and students come to the educational experience not as tabulae rasae, but rather as complex human beings with deeply held beliefs and values that can facilitate or impede the teaching/learning process (Abel, 1992).
- Multicultural education is a philosophy, a process, and an educational reform movement that uses methodologies and instructional materials to promote equity of information and high standards of academic scholarship, in an environment that respects the potential of each student. It is a restatement of sound educational pedagogy, practices, and research that requires the collective representation of all cultures and groups as significant to the accumulation of knowledge (Banks, 1994; Grant, 1992; Swartz, 1992).
- Effective instructors are those who have examined their own perceptions, biases, and behaviors related to cultural diversity, and who have a clear understanding of the origins of cultural identifications. They have a knowledge of cultural information, theory and research, as well as general interpersonal skills for communicating, negotiating, and resolving conflicts. They realize that the quality of social interaction is significant to cultural understanding (Adams, 1991; Adams & Welsch, 1994, 1995; Larke, 1992).

College professors. As more professors prepare undergraduate and graduate students to work in culturally diverse settings, they will find it necessary to develop and employ a repertoire of skills to critically evaluate their own biases that may impede their ability to foster effective multicultural teaching (Schoem, Frankel, Zuniga, & Lewis, 1995). Often, this requires a change in instructional strategy. Some suggestions for helping college professors promote instruction that helps to eradicate instructional racism are as follows:

- *The need for instructional change.* Most instructional change has been initiated by the changing demographics (among students at all levels, from pre-K to higher education), increases in immigration, and a realization that traditional instructional methods do not meet the needs of a diverse student population, nor do they adequately prepare all students to function in a culturally pluralistic society. College professors must ask themselves critical questions, such as, "Is your need motivated by 1) policies and practices in your department/college/ institution, 2) class evaluations, 3) tenure and promotion guidelines, 4) changes in teacher education programs, or 5) the results of personal experiences?" They must ask what critical beliefs, skills, and behaviors are necessary in teacher training to ensure that all teachers are prepared to teach all students. "Business as usual" will no longer suffice. If teacher educators expect teachers in training to alter pedagogical behaviors, then such changes will have to be demonstrated and modeled. Therefore, teacher educators are charged to build their own knowledge base to become more culturally responsive.

- *Critical evaluation of the role of the college professor in the teaching/learning process regarding issues about diversity.* Several critical questions should be addressed, such as: 1) Do you have an adequate knowledge base of diversity issues? 2) Does your discipline include issues about diversity? If so, how are they addressed? Is research about diversity centered around deficit theories through use of such terms as "disadvantaged," "deprived," and "dysfunctional" when explaining the conditions and participation of some ethnic groups? 3) Does your discipline support and validate the work of scholars who try to integrate the tenets of multicultural education? Are topics related to multicultural education infusion included on conference agendas? Do refereed journals include articles about multicultural education issues? Are graduate students encouraged to develop scholarly research agendas about diversity issues? Does external funding exist to promote research that develops new paradigms about diversity issues?

- *Familiarity with the multicultural education literature.* Multicultural education and multicultural teacher education are concerned with the education needs of all students, including those who are culturally, linguistically, ethnically, and economically diverse. Multicultural education is not a new phenomenon (Mills, 1983). In fact, according to Mills, the history of multicultural education can be divided into four time periods: Ethnic Saturation and Disorientation (1901-1953); Ethnic Unrest (1945-1965); Ethnic and Cultural Consciousness (1966-1973); and Reeducation, Research, and Reform in Cultural Understanding (1974-present).

According to Carl Grant, President of the National Association of Multicultural Education, multicultural education is both a philosophical concept and an educational process. It is a concept built upon the same philosophical ideals of freedom, justice, equality, equity, and human dignity that are contained in the Declaration of Independence. It recognizes, however, that equality and equity are not the same thing: equal access does not necessarily guarantee fairness. Multicultural education is a process that takes place in schools and other education institutions, and it informs all academic curriculum. It prepares all students to work actively toward structural equality in the organizations and institutions of the United States. It helps students to develop positive self-concepts, and to discover who they are, particularly in terms of their multiple group membership. Multicultural education does this by providing knowledge about the history and culture of the diverse groups that have shaped the history, politics, and culture of the United States. Multicultural education acknowledges that the strengths and richness of the United States lie in the diversity of its citizens. It demands a school staff that is multiracial and multiculturally literate, and that includes staff members who are fluent in more than one language. It demands a curriculum that organizes concepts and content around the contributions, perspectives, and experiences of the myriad groups that are part of U.S. society. It confronts and seeks to bring about change in current social issues involving race, ethnicity, socioeconomic class, gender, and disability. It accomplishes this by providing instruction in a context that students are familiar with, and by building upon students' diverse learning styles. It teaches critical thinking skills, as well as democratic decision-making, social action, and empowerment skills. Finally, multicultural education is a total process that cannot be truncated: All components of its definitions must be in place in order for multicultural education to be genuine and valuable (Grant & Ladson-Billings, 1997).

The American Association of Colleges of Teacher Education (AACTE), in its 1977 statement, "No One Model American," defined multicultural education as education that values cultural pluralism (Marshall, 1992). Multicultural education rejects the view that schools should seek to melt away cultural differences, and criticizes schools that merely tolerate cultural pluralism. Instead, multicultural education affirms that schools should be oriented toward the cultural enrichment of all children and youth through programs rooted to the preservation and extension of cultural alternatives. Beginning in 1979, institutions applying for accreditation or reaccreditation from the National Council for Accreditation of Teacher Education (NCATE) were required to show evidence of multicultural education in their teacher preparation programs. According to NCATE, multicultural education is preparation for the social, political, and economic realities of culturally diverse, complex societies. This preparation helps an individual develop competencies for behaving in different cultural settings (Marshall, 1992).

- *Participation in experiences to increase cultural awareness.* Participating in professional staff development workshops regarding issues of diversity, attending multicultural education conferences, such as the ones presented by the National Association for Multicultural Education (NAME), reading multicultural education literature, and conducting on-line computer searches are all instrumental in developing a knowledge and experience base to promote multiculturalism in your classes.
- *Revising the course syllabi to address issues of diversity.* Professors should look at their class syllabi and reflect on the following questions: What kind of multicultural activities do you promote? How do you as an instructor deal with multicultural issues? When do you discuss multicultural issues? Do you feel multicultural issues are appropriate for your course? Search the literature on the teaching/learning process and identify practices that will help you to reorganize your syllabus to reflect appropriate instructional techniques.
- *Knowledge of teaching style.* The philosophical and theoretical origins of teaching styles are grounded in the knowledge of student development and learning. The literature identifies teaching styles as "traditional or facilitating, direct or indirect,

or didactic or progressive" (see Gollnick & Chinn, 1986; Ramirez & Castaneda, 1974). As college classrooms become more diverse and students learn skills that would enable them to participate in diverse working environments, it is imperative that a college professor's teaching style match the students' learning styles.

- *Consult faculty within the college/institution who have expertise in multicultural education.* On many college campuses, the leading people in the discipline of multicultural education (ME) share their knowledge more often outside of the college/university than within their respective institutions. Their offices are filled with the most recent books, articles, research studies, and videos. Collaboration with these experts will provide much information, and can build professional relationships within institutions. Building professional relationships, however, requires give and take. Often, the ME expert is expected to attend all of the ME conferences and be the spokesperson for ME issues, while others shirk such responsibilities.

- *Promote academic inclusion.* The debate over the "canon" is causing educators to rethink course content. Research supports that curricular racism and bias ran the gamut from omissions to distortions, and from selective inclusion to selective exclusion of information (Banks & Banks, 1995). Professors should review the content of materials used in classrooms in order to ensure a variety of different perspectives. This type of teaching uses the highest level of questioning skills and encourages students to become seekers of knowledge. According to Swartz (1992), this type of teaching also requires students to critically define, analyze, and synthesize the knowledge they need, rather than merely support predetermined sets of information. Such an expansion of the knowledge base requires time, and much of this knowledge is only found in secondary sources. When faculty members and students become a community of learners, however, gathering new information can benefit all stakeholders.

Preservice and inservice teachers. Inservice teachers and preservice teachers also are in positions to lessen instructional racism. According to Larke (1992), effective multicultural teachers:

- Are sensitive to the needs of all students, and realize that the cultural congruence between teacher and student is significant to student success (Nelson-Barber & Meier, 1990; Pang, 1988)
- View differences among students in an egalitarian mode, rather than an inferior or superior mode (Gollnick & Chinn, 1986)
- Have a desire to know students' historical and cultural backgrounds, knowing that the information can increase a teacher's sensitivity and awareness, as well as provide the knowledge base to supplement instructional materials (Banks, 1989)
- Change their teaching strategies to meet the learning styles of students (Shade, 1989)
- Have high expectations of all students and provide the necessary experiences that would enable all students to meet those high expectations
- Value the need to form relationships with parents early in the school year before academic or behavioral concerns arise (Charkin, 1989; Tyler, 1989)
- Use the student's environment, regardless of economic conditions, as a spring-

board for instructional design
- Have the ability to recognize "isms" (racism, classism, sexism), both in the hidden curriculum and the formal curriculum, and make concerted efforts to minimize such inequalities in the classroom (Gollnick & Chinn, 1986)
- Possess a wealth of instructional strategies for diverse classrooms, such as cooperative grouping, mastery learning, or experiential learning (Bloom, 1988; Slavin, 1984)
- View their role as a facilitator for students outside the dominant culture by incorporating teaching and learning strategies that enable students to be successful without having to give up their cultural identity and conform to the dominant culture (Kuykendall, 1992).

We realize that instructional racism cannot be eradicated by college professors, or by elementary and secondary teachers and administrators alone. Their positions and their ability to shape the lives of students through education, however, can significantly decrease the incidence of instructional racism.

Conclusion

While instructional racism is not a new issue in education, the term, as defined here, is an emerging concept that critically examines the impact of racism within instruction. Instructional racism, then, is the existing relationship between teacher-held, intentional and common cultural prejudices, and the expressed teacher treatments of students that perpetuate a hierarchically stratified and monoculturally controlled social order. It is not the authors' intention to identify instructional racism as having an independent existence separate from the reality of racism itself. It is our unequivocal assertion, however, that instructional racism, as racism itself evidences, is a state of mind. This thinking drives individual, as well as group-selected, behaviors. We offer this definition as a cognitive starting point for any and all practitioners seeking to examine and eliminate their own personal use of such teaching beliefs and behaviors.

Healing the wounds of instructional racism is a continuous process that must be placed on political and educational agendas, and specifically in teacher education programs, as well as programs in other disciplines. Research supports that education is one of the best defenses against racism (Banks, 1994; Banks & Banks, 1995). Since college professors and elementary and secondary teachers are at the core of the education system, then their instruction *must* be free of racist values and practices. Thus, educators at all levels are in the best positions to eradicate instructional racism, while providing all students, regardless of their cultural, linguistic, ethnic, or economic diversity, the opportunities to be successful in academic environments.

References

Abel, P. (1992). A culturally responsive, gender-sensitive pedagogical model: The college teaching/learning process. In
C. Grant (Ed.), *Multicultural education for the twenty-first
century* (pp. 27-34). Proceedings of the Second Annual
Meeting of the National Association for Multicultural Education. Morristown, NJ: Paramont Publishing, Silver Burdett
Ginn, Inc.

Adams, J. Q. (1991). Understanding social interaction in the
culturally diverse classroom. In J. Q. Adams, J. Niss, & C.
Suarez (Eds.), *Multicultural education: Strategies for imple-
mentation in colleges and universities* (pp. 93-100).
Macomb, IL: Western Illinois University. Illinois Staff and
Curriculum Developers Association..

Adams, J. Q., & Welsch, J. (Eds.). (1994). *Multicultural education: Strategies for implementation in colleges and universities* (Vol. 4). Macomb, IL: Western Illinois University. Illinois
Staff and Curriculum Developers Association.

Adams, J. Q., & Welsch, J. (Eds.). (1995). *Multicultural prism:
Voices from the field.* Macomb, IL: Western Illinois University.
Illinois Staff and Curriculum Developers Association.

Artiles, A. J., & Trent, S. C. (1994). Overrepresentation of minority
students in special education: A continuous debate. *The
Journal of Special Education, 27*(4), 410-437.

Banks, J. (1989). *Multiethnic education.* Boston: Allyn and Bacon.

Banks, J. (1994). *Multiethnic education: Theory and practice* (3rd
ed.). Needman Heights, MA: Allyn and Bacon.

Banks, J., & Banks, C. (Eds.). (1995). *The handbook of research on
multicultural education.* New York: Macmillian.

Bloom, B. (1988). Helping all children learn in elementary school—
and beyond. *Principal,* 12-17.

Boykin, A. W. (1983). The academic performance of Afro-American children. In J. Spence (Ed.), *Achievement and achievement motives* (pp. 324-371). San Francisco, CA: W.H. Freeman.

Charkin, N. (1989). Debunking the myth about minority parents.
Educational Horizons, 119-123.

Delpit, L. D. (1988). The silenced dialogue: Power and pedagogy
in educating other people's children. *Harvard Educational
Review, 58,* 280-298.

Delpit, L. D. (1995). *Other people's children: Cultural conflict in the
classroom.* New York: The New Press.

Fullan, M. (1993). *Change forces: Probing the depths of educational reform.* Bristol, PA: The Falmer Press.

Garcia, E. (1994). *Understanding and meeting the challenge of
student cultural diversity.* Boston: Houghton Mifflin.

Gollnick, D., & Chinn, P. (1986). *Multicultural education in a pluralistic
society* (2nd ed.). Columbus, OH: Charles E. Merrill.

Grant, C. (1992). *Research and multicultural education: From the
margins to the mainstream.* Bristol, PA: The Falmer Press.

Grant, C., & Ladson-Billings (Eds.). (1977). *Dictionary of multicultural
education.* Phoenix, AZ: The Oryx Press.

Grossman, H. (1995). *Teaching in a diverse society.* Needham Heights,
MA: Allyn and Bacon.

Harry, B., & Anderson, M. G. (1994). The disproportionate placement of
African American males in special education programs: A critique
of the process. *Journal of Negro Education, 63*(4), 602-619.

Jones, R. L. (Ed.). (1989). *Black psychology* (3rd ed.). Berkeley, CA:
Cobb & Henry.

Kierstead, F., & Wagner, P. (1993). *The ethical, legal and multicultural
foundations of teaching.* Madison, WI: WCB Brown & Bench-

mark Publishers.

King, J. E. (1991). Dysconscious racism: Ideology, identity and the miseducation of teachers. *Journal of Negro Education, 60*(2), 133-146.

Kuykendall, C. (1992). *From rage to hope: Strategies for reclaiming Black and Hispanic students.* Bloomington, IN: National Educational Service.

Ladson-Billings, G. (1994). *The dreamkeepers.* San Francisco, CA: Jossey-Bass Publishers.

Larke, P. J. (1992). Effective multicultural teachers: Meeting the challenges of diverse classrooms. *Equity & Excellence, 25,* 133-138.

Marshall, P. L. (1992). *Toward a theoretical framework for the design of multicultural education in teacher education programs.* A paper presented to the College and University Faculty Assembly of the National Council for the Social Studies at the 72nd Annual Meeting, Detroit, MI.

Mills, J. (1983). Multicultural education: Where do we go from here? *Journal of Social and Behavioral Sciences, 25,* 43-52.

Nelson-Barber, S., & Meier, T. (1990). Multicultural context a key factor in teaching. *Academic Corrections,* 1-5.

Nichols, E. J. (1976). *Cultural foundations of teaching Black children.* Proceedings of World Psychiatric Association of Psychiatrists in Nigeria Conference. University of Ibadab, Nigeria.

Nieto, S. (1996). *Affirming diversity: The sociopolitical context of multicultural education.* New York: Longman.

Omi, M., & Winant, H. (1994). *Racial formation in the United States* (2nd ed.). New York: Routledge.

Pang, V. O. (1988). Ethnic prejudice: Still alive and hurtful. *Harvard Educational Review, 58*(3), 375-379.

Payne, R. K. (1995). *A framework: Understanding and working with students and adults from poverty.* Baytown, TX: RFT Publishing.

Ramirez, M., & Castaneda, A. (1974). *Cultural democracy, bicognitive development and education.* New York: Academic Press.

Schoem, D., Frankel, L., Zuniga, X., & Lewis, E. (1995). *Multicultural teaching in the university.* Westport, CT: Praeger Publishers.

Shade, B. J. (1989). *Culture, style and the educative process.* Springfield, IL: Charles C. Thomas.

Slavin, R. (1984). Students motivating students to excel: Cooperative incentives, cooperative tasks, and student achievement. *Elementary School Journal,* 53-65.

Swartz, E. (1992). Multicultural education: From a compensatory to a scholarly foundation. In C. Grant (Ed.), *Research and multicultural education: From the margins to the mainstream* (pp. 32-43). Washington, DC: The Falmer Press.

Takaki, R. (1993). *A different mirror: A history of multicultural America.* Boston: Little, Brown.

Tyler, R. (1989). Educating children from minority families. *Educational Horizons,* 114-118.

U.S. Department of Education, National Center for Education Statistics. (1995). *The conditions of education, 1995.* (NCES No. 95-272). Washington, DC: Author.

U.S. Department of Education. (1996). To assure the free and appropriate public education for all handicapped children. *18th Annual Report to Congress on the Implementation of the Handicapped Act.* Washington, DC: Author.

Wellman, D. T. (1993). *Portraits of white racism* (2nd ed.). Cambridge: Cambridge University Press.

Williams, C. (1987). *The destruction of Black civilization.* Chicago, IL: Third World Press.

Woodson, C. G. (1933). *The mis-education of the Negro.* New York: Amsterdam Press.

chapter IV

Family Involvement: Empowering Families To Heal Racism

Phyllis Y. Hammonds, *West Helena, Arkansas*
Cathy Gutierrez-Gomez, *University of New Mexico*

As society becomes increasingly more diverse, we educators interact with students, colleagues, families, and others who think, talk, walk, look, and even celebrate holidays in many different ways. How do we perceive them? Do we judge their cultural values against our own? Do we look for sameness and understanding? Do we ignore differences and hope they go away? If we ignore these differences, do we create learning environments that are conducive for growth and development, regardless of the learner's race, creed, culture, and/or natural origin?

Why is it essential for educators to understand cultural diversity and racism? Educators bring their own "baggage"—personal life experiences—related to cultural diversity and racial issues to classrooms and other education settings. These values and beliefs are shaped by families and communities during early childhood and they affect how educators work with students, colleagues, and/or families of different cultural groups. Whether in child care settings or graduate school, all learners need the benefit of tolerant and healthful learning environments if they are to develop to their fullest potential. More important, young children need these environments to develop a sense of self and to develop "positive attitudes" (Gestwicki, 1996, p. 316) toward people who are different from them. Such a rich learning environment benefits everyone—the educator, learner, family, and community—and gives learners the confidence to challenge racial injustices and become productive citizens. In the absence of tolerance, learners suffer.

When racial/cultural conflict arises between the educator and the family, it is disturbing and confusing for children (Gestwicki, 1996). In this chapter, Cathy, an American Indian/Mexican American and one of the authors, shares her family's story. Her 5-year-old son was dismissed from his kindergarten class in a suburban school because of his long hair. Cathy recounts how this episode affected her family, focusing on her children's resultant emotional stress. When educators fully comprehend how to build partnerships with families, they will be able to bridge the cultural gap between home and school, perhaps reducing the frequency of such harmful conflicts.

How can educators empower families to heal racism? It is not easy. As a matter of fact, the journey is long, tedious, and often lonesome. We offer these basic suggestions:

Basic Steps for Educators

First Step: Confront your own racist and stereotypical "demons." These are your personal biases and prejudices. Contrary to what some educators think, everyone has them. In other words, everyone is prejudiced against something or someone. It is not a myth, but a reality—racism is alive and well (see empowerment approach: personal level, pp. 77 for more details.)

Second Step: Become culturally sensitive by learning about different cultures. In the process, you can serve as a model for students, families, colleagues, and others in the community. While educators do not have to know everything about every cultural group, they should learn enough to value, respect, and understand both cultural differences and similarities.

Educators must develop knowledge about cultural diversity, and learn about racism and its harmful effects. Why is this necessary? This knowledge is a prerequisite for eradicating racism. When educators become knowledgeable, they are empowered to mentor others to challenge racism.

Third Step: Do not make racist comments and/or perform racial acts against anyone. When we hear or witness racial acts, our brains should immediately send signals to our "antennas," causing them to quiver, and then send "chills" down our backs, causing us to shake. These quivers and shakes may indicate we are culturally sensitive, perhaps provoking "sensitive" educators to counter such racist acts (see empowerment approach: political level, pp. 83).

Fourth Step: Develop partnerships with families and communities to learn about other cultures. This is essential if we are to prepare children to live in a multicultural society (Hopson, Hopson, & Clavin, 1993). Educators owe this to children, who, after all, represent our future. Also, form partnerhsips to gain knowledge and support, and serve as a mentor and advocate against racial injustices (see empowerment approach: interpersonal level, pp. 80).

Why are such partnerships essential? When teachers and families develop a partnership, everyone benefits—the child, the family, and the community. These partnerships are based on mutual trust and respect, and they help to bridge the cultural gap between the home and school. How do teachers build such partnerships? It is not easy. Some educators are uncomfortable and unsure about developing partnerships with families of different cultural groups, because they have no experience doing so. Therefore, many do not know where to begin. This attitude creates a barrier—an atmosphere of mistrust—and promotes conflict between teacher and family.

A starting point for partnerships is learning about each individual family—their traditions, customs, beliefs, values, and practices. This starts early, before the learner enters the classroom door, and it may continue for a lifetime. A "family-friendly" and culturally sensitive learning environment must be created by classroom teachers. They should *ask* families how they want to become involved in their child's educational life—not *tell* them how. This may be accomplished by conducting surveys and having informal conversations during home visits, teacher/parent conferences, etc.

After teachers and families become partners, they may feel more secure posing questions regarding racial issues. Parents may ask for assistance on how to address these issues with their children. Empowered educators should know where to go for information and resources; for example, they may want to conduct (with families) a series of workshops, using the framework suggested in this chapter.

Since all families are unique and different, it is important to start building partnerships where the family is and not where we want them to be (see Barbour & Barbour, 1997; Barclay & Boone, 1995; U.S. Department of Health and Human Services, 1998). We must respect their right to self-determination and to make choices. When partnerships are established between educators and families, both parties may feel more comfortable in sharing their own family stories, culture, and history. This is how we, the authors, who are former co-workers, became close friends. Our dialogue on racial issues began with the question, "What do you want to be called?" Translated, this means, "What term do you use to identify your racial/ethnic identity?" This question empowered us to share our innermost thoughts and feelings regarding how we and our families dealt with, and are dealing with, racial issues. For over 10 years, we have been partners to healing racism.

Fifth Step: Become an advocate to fight racism and create an inclusive and fair society. Educators must begin fighting racism in their own "backyards"—their homes, communities, and institutions, etc. Of course, speaking out and fighting racism is a complex and tedious task. It is a necessity, however, in order to effect social and economic change (see pp. 83) for those who are oppressed.

This chapter opens with true stories of racial incidents. We recount these riveting stories to reveal how our families of color—one African American and the other American Indian/Mexican American—encountered and survived the "ugly scars" of racism. Following these stories, we present a Multidimensional Empowerment Approach to healing racism. Initially, this approach was specifically designed for families. Teachers can adapt it for personal use and/or to develop a series of workshops.

Racism: 1960s Style

(Scene: A crowded bus station in the South.)
"We don't serve colored folks."
"I just want to buy two coca-colas."
"I can't sell you coca-colas."
"But my children and I are thirsty! It's hot and they need something cold to drink!"
"Lady, you heard me—we don't serve colored folks!"
"Children, they won't sell us a coke."
"Well, Mama, what do we do?"
"Go back to the bus!"

Imagine my mother, Mrs. Thelma Helen Hammonds, a 30-something African American woman, attempting to buy two colas in a crowded bus station filled with White people in the 1960s. Do you feel my mother's pain as the White man refused to sell her two ice cold colas? My mother, a 6th-grade teacher, could not believe this was happening to her. Do you feel the heat on this hot southern summer day and the "heat" that "burns" between the oppressors and the oppressed?

"We don't serve colored folks." The White man's voice loudly echoed in Mrs. Hammonds's ear and throughout the entire crowded bus station, causing everyone to stop and stare. "All eyes were upon me," remembers Mrs. Hammonds, "the evil White man, the customers, our bus driver, and fellow White passengers, who said nothing in our defense. I knew what they were saying about us because their piercing eyes told the story. 'What are you doing here, n———-?'"

Back in the 1960s, racism often took such brutal and overt forms as lynching, beatings, and cross burning (Franklin & Moss, 1980). Prior to the 1960s civil rights legislation, this type of racial incident was commonplace for many families of color, more specifically African American families. It was the "in your face" kind of racism that the South did not care to hide. Through Jim Crow laws, southerners excluded and/or separated African Americans from public facilities such as restrooms, movie theaters, schools, and restaurants. The 1964 Civil Rights Act banned such discrimination in public facilities (Bell, 1992).

My mother and I continue to hear the "voices" and feel the "heat" of that racial incident. Although this incident occurred over three decades ago, it is still a fresh memory in our minds (my younger sister, Adrian, does not recall it) because racism hurts and hurts. It runs deep and has lasting effects. Moreover, it saps one's energy—sometimes, even the life—of its victims. Racist acts leave victims feeling powerless while the perpetrators feel powerful, as demonstrated in this illustration provided by my mother:

"If looks could kill, I would have died—right there in that bus station. My only desire was to treat you girls to cold coca-colas on a hot summer day. Nothing more! No one stood up for us. No one challenged the White man, not even [the] White passengers who had befriended us during our bus trip. But that's the way things were back in the '60s."

Fortunately, my family's wounds are healing. However, our scars—"the permanent markers" of the past—still remain. To heal these scars and to effect social change, my mother, sister, and I are advocates in our various communities. We speak, write, and act against ugly racist acts. Also, we share our stories and offer suggestions to younger family members and other interested persons on how to "survive and rise" when racism strikes. These suggestions are based on lessons learned from this and other racial encounters throughout the years. Maya Angelou (1994) eloquently describes this effort in one of her most popular poems, "Still I Rise."

You may write me down in history
with your bitter, twisted lies,
You may trod me in the very dirt
But still, like dirt, I'll rise
. . . Out of the hurts of history's shame
I rise
Up from a past that's rooted in pain
I rise . . .

My passion to promote racial harmony and solidarity is a lifelong commitment. I am a community activist who works tirelessly to combat racism and injustices in my community and wherever I go. As I read and study incessantly about this subject, my approach to combating racism is evolving. Workshops and conferences offered at colleges and universities and organizations such as the Anti-Defamation League of B'nai B'rith are empowering—they are shaping my attitude and behavior toward racial issues.

My mother, now a retired educator, is optimistic about the status of racial affairs in our community and in our nation. She is making a difference by serving on various multiethnic committees in her community that promote racial unity. Also, she attends community and social functions that include people from all walks of life. Thirty years ago in this segregated southern community, African Americans were not invited to attend such events as political rallies, store grand openings, city-sponsored events, etc. Today, my mother believes her involvement in such events is a small but significant step toward bridging the gap between two worlds—one Black and one White. She states, "I'm working to make the future brighter for my grandchildren and others of their generation. Perhaps racism will end in the next century—for my great-grandchildren!"

My sister Adrian has experienced numerous racial conflicts—as a student and an adult. As a mother of two children, she shares her stories of these racial conflicts, considering them teaching tools to help her children cope with their concerns regarding racism. They read books and magazines that promote racial unity and that discuss people of different racial and ethnic groups. Adrian is a high school science teacher. Whenever a racial conflict occurs in her class, she immediately discusses its harmful effects with her students and perceives this as a "teachable moment," although some of her students disagree with this approach.

In addition, Adrian uses an array of resources to educate her students regarding the contributions of scientists and inventors of different racial and ethnic groups. Frequently, she gives extra points for research on this topic. According to my sister, this helps broaden her students' knowledge about the contributions of people of color to American society.

Unfortunately, racism will follow my family into the 21st century. Of course, we are disappointed because this means our fight against racism must continue. We never dreamt this would be the case. Racism is a horrible nightmare without an ending. According to a friend, "it [racism] is worse than a nightmare because [with a nightmare] at least you can wake up and it's over, but honey, racism—after you wake up—goes on and on. It's never over." Every so often, I feel the same way.

Today, as in the 1960s, racism is an issue. As our nation becomes increasingly more racially and ethnically diverse, racial groups compete for power and control. Such competition often leads to violence, destruction, and sometimes death (Holman, 1994). Sadly, the rich diversity in the United States has only led to division. Racism's resurgence is a shocking revelation to those Americans who thought it ended in the 1960s, to those who deny its existence, and to those who ignore it.

Media reports of vicious racial acts are shattering America's hopes for racial unity and peace—now and in the future. Kweisi Mfume (personal communication, 1997), President of the NAACP, states that "Today's acts of racial violence and intimidation are a nightmarish repetition [of] the past." He is encouraging interested Americans to unite in a fight against racism with the same vigor as in the past. President Clinton is also deeply concerned about America's racial divide—he calls it "America's constant curse"—and views racism as the challenge of our past and a "challenge of our future" ("Blacks at the Inaugural," 1997). During his second inaugural speech, the President pleaded for America to celebrate its diversity, and to unite and heal racial divisiveness before the 21st century.

In 1997, President Clinton formulated a multi-ethnic advisory board to investigate, and advise him regarding, the status of race relations in America. John Hope Franklin, a noted historian and author, chaired this board. ("White House Names Advisory Board on Race," 1997). This board released a final report titled, "One America in the 21st Century: Forging a New Future." It is a summary of the board's experiences and recommendations to improve race relations in the new century. One salient point of this report reveals that "discrimination on the basis of race, color and ethnicity continues to be a fact of life in America" (United States Information Agency, 1998). Will Congress and American citizens support this report and join President Clinton in efforts to eradicate racism? This question is still "up in the air." Soon after the report's release, some civil rights activists and conservatives indicated they were disappointed with its recommendations, while others praised it (Fletcher, 1998). What will America do? Will racism, a "hideous curse," follow us into the new millennium?

America's survival depends upon how its citizens get along. As Rodney King, the famous victim of a beating by Los Angeles police, said, "Why can't we get along?" Five years later, President Clinton asked some similar questions in his second inaugural address: "Will we be one nation, one people with one common destiny or not? Will we all come together or come apart?" ("Blacks at the Inaugural," 1997). The authors of this chapter believe that it is time to stop asking questions and time to take action!

Racism:
1990s Style

According to Elizabeth Martinez, a Chicana activist, racism affects not only blacks, but also brown people. She further indicates that there are "multiple forms" of racism, specifically for people of Mexican descent. These include several "components," such as skin color and other physical features, culture, language, and legal status (Lyon, 1997, p. 15). Moreover, she advocates that people of color should join forces to fight these forms of racism and social inequality. As an African American, I agree with Ms. Martinez—for there is "strength in numbers." Cathy, the co-author of this chapter, and I find this strategy an effective tool for dealing with racial conflicts and other pertinent issues that affect our personal and professional lives. Our alliance has helped us build a strong and close friendship that has lasted for nearly 20 years.

Cathy Gutierrez-Gomez is a college professor at the University of New Mexico in Albuquerque. In this section, she describes her son's suspension from kindergarten, for having long hair, at a suburban school near Dallas, Texas. This is an example of racism based on "physical features." Cathy vividly describes how this racial/cultural conflict affected her family, the school, the community, and the nation. This case gained national exposure through news articles and during Linda Ellerbee's report on

"Nick News" on the Nickelodeon Cable Channel (1992). Again, this family emerged empowered and willing to challenge racism.

Some questions to consider while reading this case study include:

What can I do to promote racial harmony?

How do I talk to my children about racism?

When do I begin my discussions about racism?

If I talk about racism, will this make my child prejudiced or racist?

Where do I go for assistance to learn how to talk to my children about this topic?

How do I adequately prepare my children to confront racism at school and in our community?

Case Example
The Gomez Family:
Cultural Conflict in a School Setting

Background Information. My family moved to a suburb of Dallas, Texas, in 1986. We had bought a new house in the area after inquiring about the school district and determining that it was considered to be one of the best. At the time of the move, our daughter, Dulce, was 2 years old; our son, Golden Eagle, was born a month later.

My husband, Greg, was determined to teach our children about their cultural heritage and instill in them a sense of pride. Our family, well-known and respected within the American Indian community, was involved in various community efforts. Greg, a Lipan and Mescalero Apache, had served on several boards and numerous committees on behalf of Indian people. I come from Huastec (Mexican Indian) and Spanish heritage, and was involved in several projects that addressed cultural awareness and sensitivity. Both my husband and I have master's degrees, and I was working on a doctorate at that time.

The Case. The summer before Golden Eagle was to start kindergarten, my husband and I became aware that the school district had a very strict dress code regarding hair length for boys. Golden Eagle had long hair and normally wore it in a single ponytail braid, like his dad. Although we did not anticipate any problems, Greg and I decided to contact school administrators to make sure our son's hair would not be an issue. After several inquiries, my family was finally informed that this matter would have to be addressed by the school board. Golden Eagle was allowed to attend kindergarten while the board reviewed the case. It seemed to us that this was probably standard procedure and that everything would work out fine.

In the meantime, Golden Eagle was thoroughly enjoying his first weeks of school and all of his new friends. Prior to starting school, Golden Eagle had dreamed of what it would be like to go to school, and often played "school" with his sister. He was quite disappointed when he turned 5 in November, only to find out he had to wait another year before he could start school. He had imagined that once he turned 5 he would be in school the very next day.

My son's first school experience changed dramatically after only five weeks. When it appeared that the school board was going to enforce the dress code, Greg and I asked to be on the agenda at the next board meeting. We felt that we could present a strong case. After all, both of us had been actively involved in efforts to promote cultural understanding and harmony.

The school board meeting started out with formal introductions, after which my husband and I asked our children to wait in the hallway where a family friend could watch them. As the board remained seated behind their long tables, we stood facing them. Greg began speaking of the importance of intercultural understanding and explained our family's beliefs and practices. He talked about his feelings for his country and the pride our family felt about being Americans. Soon, some of the school board members were asking questions. They did not understand why keeping Golden Eagle's hair long was more important than conforming to the school district's 27-year-old policy.

As the meeting continued, Greg and I shared with the board that this would be our fourth year at the school. We had been active in PTA and all the school functions. We knew Dulce's teachers and had volunteered in the classroom and at special functions. Both Dulce and her little brother were quite familiar with the school and the people there. All of Dulce's friends and most of the neighborhood children attended the same school.

Greg and I stood before the school board for an hour, answering questions and attempting to respond to the superintendent and board members, who wanted to know why we "couldn't be like everybody else and just follow the rules." The board issued a waiver that allowed Golden Eagle to attend kindergarten while they studied the hair issue. A few weeks later, Greg and I were informed that a special board meeting was scheduled for us. We arrived at the meeting site and were surprised to find the large meeting room filled with about 50 school administrators, teachers, and some parents. Several individuals spoke on behalf of the school district, each strongly supporting the importance of following the district's rules and regulations.

It was evident to Greg and me that the board had already made its decision. A quick vote was called for and the decision was now official; the hair policy would be enforced. That night, Greg and I tried to explain to our children what this decision meant. Both of them were confused and angry, they couldn't understand why this was happening. My family decided Golden Eagle would go to school for the rest of the week and demand that the school district make alternate arrangements.

The school district did not respond until that Friday, when the school principal was asked to inform us that Golden Eagle would not be allowed to return to class on Monday unless he cut his hair. I was confronted with the news after dropping Golden Eagle off in his classroom. I demanded an explanation from the principal, who simply stated that he was just following orders. Dulce, who had come to hug me good-bye, was standing to the side, crying. She had heard everything. The principal continued to state the conditions that we would have to follow if Golden Eagle was to return the following week. Dulce's teachers tried to comfort her and reassure her that things would work out.

After much discussion and soul-searching, Greg and I went to the school at noon to pick up our children. By this time, many supporters had found out what was happening; about 30 people showed up at the school to show their support. It was also at this time that the parents and children in Golden Eagle's class became aware of what was happening. The parents were surprised and bewildered. Our son's classmates did not understand what was happening.

The news media had followed the story after the first board meeting and they were interviewing people outside the school. People from the community were appalled that a little boy was being kicked out of kindergarten for wearing his hair in a culturally traditional fashion. It was evident that my family had strong community support. The phone calls and letters that followed reiterated the support from local, state, and national sympathizers.

Greg and I filed a lawsuit against the school district and spent a year gathering evidence and responding to inquiries from school district lawyers. During this time, I home-schooled Golden Eagle. Because he wanted to be in a school with children his age, I later enrolled him in an adjoining school district. Dulce finished 3rd grade at the only school she had ever known. My family made plans to move and enroll the children in another suburban school district.

A year later, I took the children for a physical exam because they both were complaining of headaches and stomachaches. They also had trouble sleeping and were wetting their beds. Their physician found no physical abnormalities and concluded that the children were responding to the stress caused by the incident with the school and the pending lawsuit. She offered us advice on how to help the children deal with the stress, and she continued to monitor their physical progress.

After an emotional family meeting, Greg and I decided to drop the lawsuit and concentrate on helping Dulce and Golden Eagle regain a sense of security and stability. We sold our home and moved, in the hopes of providing our children with a positive school experience. My family will never forget this incident and the emotional turmoil it brought. My husband and I have continued our involvement in efforts to bring about cultural understanding and harmony.

Reflective Questions:
- What are a family's rights in a situation when their cultural and traditional values are in conflict with school district policies?
- What are the school district's rights in the same situation?
- Is there a process that could lead both parties to an amicable solution?
- Is the school district in any way responsible for the trauma the children experienced?
- What can people do to prevent this type of discord between home and school?

MULTIDIMENSIONAL EMPOWERMENT APPROACH FOR FAMILIES TO HEAL RACISM

The Multidimensional Empowerment Approach described here may support teachers of young children to empower families to develop positive racial attitudes. Although this approach was specifically designed for families, it is flexible enough to serve as a practical framework for any person interested in understanding and healing racism. Teachers should use this framework to fit the specific needs and interests of their students' families. A series of interactive workshops covering each level must be carefully planned over a period of time (i.e., three months, six months, one year). Forming planning committees will help in delegating responsibility for specific tasks. Workshop planners should remember to include teachers, families, and members of the community. These individuals may provide support, services, and resources. Also, these people will be helpful with the implementation and evaluation of these activities and other related areas. Conduct these activities in a variety of settings.

Some families may not be able to participate. Therefore, we recommend home activities and/or "home bags" to complete at their convenience.

We hope this empowerment approach will enable families and educators to work as partners to help children and themselves gain the necessary skills and knowledge to combat racism. We believe family involvement is crucial to the healing process, because it is the institution where racism begins and where it should end. "The ultimate goal is for families to stand up individually or with others to eradicate racism within their families, communities, and the world" (Ford, 1994).

Each level presents tasks for families to discover, perform, discuss, investigate, and enjoy as a family unit or independently. Families may feel free to add or delete any tasks and suggestions.

The Personal Level is first—its theme is "Know Thyself and Family." This self-awareness level is extremely important, because families need to develop positive self-esteem if they are to heal racism. Low self-esteem often leads to racist and preju-dicial attitudes (Hopson & Hopson, 1990). Families need to examine how they feel about themselves and each other. Other areas for discussion and discovery include racial/ethnic identity, cultural heritage, origins of racism/prejudices, and racial attitudes (Mathias & French, 1996). This self-discovery process helps families to develop pride, reshape their views on racism, gain confidence, and develop a family vision statement to eradicate racism (Ford, 1994).

The Interpersonal Level, "Informing and Influencing Others," stresses the acquisition of specific knowledge and skills to understand how racism works, and to learn about differ-ent forms of racism and how they affect people. With this knowledge, the family becomes more capable of informing and influencing others to join the struggle against racism.

The last and highest point of this Empowerment Approach to heal racism is the Politi-cal Level, titled "We Shall Overcome!" It is analogous to Maslow's self-actualization level on his hierarchy of human needs (Department of Health and Human Service, 1980). At this level, the family is confident, knowledgeable, and empowered to stand up and fight racism alone or with others. They become activists in the movement to end racism.

As families progress though these levels, we suggest that they collaborate with individuals who may serve as mentors for moral support, guidance, and information. These individuals may be family, friends, co-workers, and/or members of oppressed groups who are actively involved in the movement (Sleeter, 1992).

The theoretical framework for this approach evolves from the social work practice described in an article titled "Empowerment and Latinos: Implications for Practice," written by Lorraine M. Gutierrez (1994-95). This approach enables individuals, families, and communities to develop the power, skills, and influence necessary to change the course of their lives. It is rooted in several human service fields, includ-ing social work, mental health, health, and education and empowerment. Gutierrez's empowerment approach focuses on the conditions of power and powerlessness and how these conditions affect people. Power is defined and expressed in various ways, deriving from several sources and existing in two forms: negative and positive.

Positive power enables people to change the course of their lives, which leads to self-worth and enhances their ability to work with others. It also helps them gain access to public policy institutions, where their voices can be heard.

Negative power prevents some groups from full participation in these institutions. This negative power often is associated with racism, which can be defined as any attitude, action, or practice, backed up by institutional power, that subordinates people because of their color or ethnic identity. Racism also is the imposition of one ethnic group's culture in such a way that it withholds respect for, demeans, or destroys the cultures of other races (Derman-Sparks & ABC Task Force, 1989).

Inherent in both types of power are issues of control, and the exclusion of specific groups. In negative power, stigmatized groups are not specifically described; however, this may mean people of color, the poor, women, etc. Meanwhile, the focus of the Empowerment Approach is to empower these stigmatized individuals, as well as other concerned individuals who want to challenge and eradicate racism. As the authors present each empowerment level, Cathy will provide updates on her family.

In addition, each level incorporates the works of Derman-Sparks & the ABC Task Force (1989), Ford (1994), Hopson, Hopson, and Clavin (1993), Mathias and French (1996), and Sleeter (1992), to offer practical ideas and tips for healing racism.

First Level:
Personal Empowerment, Self-Discovery
"Know Thyself" Before Teaching Someone Else!

This first level offers families practical tips for conducting self-examinations regarding their self-esteem and racial attitudes. "I began to understand self-esteem isn't everything; it's just that there's nothing without it" (Steinem, 1992).

According to Hopson & Hopson (1990), parents must examine their own insecurities and attitudes regarding racial issues before they discuss them with their children. They must first "look in the mirror" to confront how they feel about themselves and their own racial views. Although racism is a difficult topic to discuss, Hopson and Hopson believe it is extremely important to do so. They classify racism as an "emotional disease"; if it is not discussed, parents are jeopardizing their children's emotional well-being (Hopson, Hopson, & Clavin, 1993).

Step 1: Self-esteem examination.
How's my self-esteem?
Mirror, Mirror, what do I see?
How do I feel about me?
What do I like or dislike about me?
Do I feel comfortable about my looks?
How do my children feel about themselves?
Am I a positive role model for my children?

Before one accepts others of a different race and culture, one must accept, feel comfortable with, and respect oneself (Hopson, Hopson, & Clavin, 1993). This acceptance of one's self is crucial to healing racism. Why? Because people who do not feel good about themselves are vulnerable to racist attitudes. A variety of terms are used to define self-esteem. It is most commonly defined as self-pride, belief in oneself, and self-respect. In this context, we prefer the Hopson and Hopson (1990) definition: Self-esteem is the feeling children (and, of course, adults) have about their self-images. Also, according to Hopson and Hopson (1990), since people usually experience bouts of both negative and positive feelings (i.e., low and high self-esteem), self-esteem refers to the self-view one has of oneself most of the time.

How is your self-view? Do you have more negative feelings than positive? If so, what is causing these negative feelings? Are these feelings emanating from you? Are these feelings caused by external sources such as friends, family, or others? According to Hopson, Hopson, and Clavin (1993), it is best to divide these problem sources into two categories: internal and external sources. The internal problems are manageable simply because it is easier to change oneself than to tackle the world—that comes with experience. Therefore, to heal racism, start with the self. Your goal is to create a positive self-view of yourself—at least most of the time.

Step 2: "Look at me and what do I see?" Eliminate self-deprecating remarks from your vocabulary, such as, "I cannot do anything right," or "My skin color is too pale or too dark." Replace them with more acceptable positive remarks about yourself, accentuating what is good about yourself, such as, "My skin color is me—it defines who I am!" Also learn to respect yourself, your family, and others, because disrespecting others is an indicator of low self-esteem. Also, recognize that bragging, constantly seeking praise from others, or exaggerating one's achievements, connections, or wealth is another example of poor regard for oneself. People who suffer from low self-esteem find ways to exhibit their superiority by projecting their personal problems on others, such as blaming a job loss on a minority group (Ford, 1994), or by committing hate crimes and gang violence (Duvall, 1994; Dyson, 1996). These disturbing acts of violence are creating havoc in America. Sadly, many of our youth are both the victims and perpetrators of this violence. According to experts on gang violence and hate crimes, these youth join gangs seeking love, security, confidence, and respect from their peers and others. They also join to destroy.

This self-examination process should become an increasingly important part of being a parent. America can no longer afford the consequences of children who grow up to hate and destroy themselves and others. Instead, we must love, nurture, protect, and respect our own and all children. To get a closer look at your "self-view," carefully examine yourself from head to toe. Ask yourself, "Am I okay?" If you are experiencing problems, don't fret—think positive thoughts and make a commitment to do something about them. To enhance your self-esteem, you may choose the "do it yourself plan" by reading self-help/improvement and motivational books and magazine articles, listening to motivational audiotapes, and exercising. Your local library is an excellent resource for materials on this subject. If you have not already, secure a library card for all your family members.

Also, consult with your physician, religious/spiritual leader, or a mental health professional, such as a family therapist or psychologist. In some communities, state-funded agencies provide mental health services at no cost or at nominal fees. For further information, consult your local yellow pages. Sometimes, removing yourself from negative situations and/or negative people may enhance your life. Remember, parents, you cannot help your children until you help yourself. As your children's first and most important teachers, it is your responsibility to nurture and foster their positive self-esteem, so that they are equipped to counter the internal and external forces that may hinder their self-development.

Step 3: Provide the basic 4 for your children. You can nurture and foster positive self-esteem in your children by providing food (good, nutritious, well-balanced meals); clothing (remember, designer clothes are not a prerequisite for a positive self-esteem); shelter (a clean, safe, hazard-free environment, with a special place your child can call his/her own); and love (lots of hugs, praises, positive reinforcement, support, discipline, nurturing, and quality time).

Numerous books on the market offer practical advice and tips on how to help children develop positive self-esteem. Be sure to select the one that best meets your and your child's interests. As previously mentioned, you also may want to seek the advice of a professional counselor.

Step 4: Explore your family's racial/ethnic background. Another aspect of self-discovery is exploring your family's racial/ethnic background (Mathias & French, 1996). How does your family "categorize" itself on the U.S. Census form? Is this relevant to your self-image? How does your family feel about its racial/ethnic identity? Every family is unique and different and must celebrate its racial/ethnic identity. This should occur before you celebrate someone else's "uniqueness." Learn about your ancestors' origins. Parents can:

- Create a family genealogy tree, with their children's involvement
- Discuss with their children the importance of knowing and respecting their cultural heritage
- Go to the local library to find adult and children's books and/or magazines that discuss family genealogy (ask the librarians for assistance with this and with how to research family roots)
- Attend family reunions, and encourage children to interview family members to help create an oral history of the family (capture these stories on videotape and audiotape)
- Create a storybook album to tell the visual story of the family (remember to date every picture and write the names of the persons in the pictures)
- Compile a family history book to share with relatives and friends
- Celebrate and record family birthdays, anniversaries, family reunions, and cultural celebrations; discuss their origins and purposes with children so they will pass this legacy to their own children
- Create a family Web site that includes favorite pictures, songs, poetry, audio sound bites, etc. to share and celebrate family uniquenesses
- Create an oral history by videotaping and/or audiotaping favorite family stories
- Use the World Wide Web to investigate the family genealogy
- Create a Web site to announce and record family reunions and other significant celebrations
- Share the family's story with the community by submitting an article to your local newspaper.

Step 5: Explore your family's racial attitudes and racial history. Prejudice and racism affect all families (Mathias & French, 1996). Therefore, it is important for you to examine your family's racial history and racial attitudes—as oppressor and/or victim. This is a difficult step that may cause you to recall painful past racist encounters, and reshape your thinking about different racial groups and the way your parents taught you. This exploration period will help you eliminate traditional racist and/or prejudicial patterns. Families may address the following questions:

- How did you learn about your racial/ethnic group?
- How did your parents and other family members feel about people of different racial/ethnic groups?
- Did your family speak openly about racism?
- How and when did you develop your racial views?
- What are the stereotypes of your racial/ethnic group? (Derman-Sparks & ABC Task Force, 1989)

These questions will help you better understand the underlying reasons for your family's perceptions.

The Final Step: Creating a family vision statement to heal. This final step is the development of a vision statement to heal racism, the development of which should involve the entire family. It is a creative expression of your family's beliefs regarding its commitment to heal racism in the world. The format is your choice. You may choose to write a poem, song, or a story. Whatever you choose, review and update your vision statement periodically as your family becomes more knowledgeable about racism. Display your vision statement in a prominent place where all can read it (Ford, 1994).

What's Happening on the Personal Level With the Gomez Family?

"Know Thyself." My family continues to live a traditional American life and to practice both our social and sacred ceremonies. Golden Eagle's hair is still as long as it ever was, as is common for many among the Apache people. Now more than ever, it has become crucial for my children to reaffirm their cultural heritage. We have made several trips to Mexico with my father to visit family and learn more about my Huastec Indian heritage. My husband, Greg, and I have continued our personal growth by attending local gatherings that promote understanding of other Indian groups from the Americas and by continuing to do research on my own and other Indian nations. In addition, Greg is keeping traditional stories alive as he practices the role of a storyteller.

Second Level: Interpersonal Empowerment "Informing and Influencing Others"

After "self-discovery," your family is ready to tackle the next level—the Interpersonal Level. At this level, you acquire the requisite empowerment knowledge and skills to understand how racism works, identify its different forms, and recognize the effects it has on people and public institutions. It also encourages your family to become acquainted (if it is not already) with people from different racial/ethnic groups, and to join support groups and organizations that support racial harmony. This is a prerequisite for encouraging others to join the movement against racism.

Step 1: Learn about racism. "Understanding racism will better equip you to take steps to eliminate it" (Ford, 1994). Do you know racism when you see it? Have you been a victim of a racist act or have you been the perpetrator of a racist act? Racism destroys both people and nations. Bosnia and Rwanda, where "ethnic-cleansing" exists, are examples of how such massive destruction affects not only a nation's people, but also the world. Will racism destroy the United States, too?

In your quest to become an empowered person, you must understand racism's causes and effects. Also, it is essential to differentiate among the terms related to cultural diversity, such as "stereotype," "discrimination," "scapegoat," "bias," "cultural," and "prejudice."

Racism causes individuals to feel superior and powerful over others (Holman, 1994). These feelings may lead to hatred and violence. Some examples of racism are as follows:

- A White person tells an African American, "I wish all African Americans were like you."
- An African American who lives in a predominantly African American community calls the police department when her home is robbed, but no one ever arrives to follow up.
- Two White parents tie their child's African American playmate to a tree and point a rifle to his head after accusing him of stealing.
- Racist/ethnic jokes and stories.
- A person says, "All those Mexicans are lazy—they don't like to work and don't care about school either."

Today's version of racism differs from the racism of the past. Racism has different faces and forms (Lyon, 1997). It is more covert than overt, which makes it more difficult to discern. Previously, racism was generally more recognizable. Also, different elements come into play, including skin color, culture, language, legal status, and physical features. Some African Americans who are members of the "Hip-Hop" generation think that the older generation believes that they don't experience racism, because it is more subtle and harder to discern . . . "because I don't have to sit on the back of the bus [older people believe that] . . . racism is gone and our generation is on easy street" (Leland & Samuels, 1997, p. 55). It isn't that simple.

Yes, racism persists. To better understand racism, conduct the following tasks:

- Watch TV and identify any racist and/or stereotypical comments, movies, news stories, etc. Keep a journal of these events. Discuss this with your family.
- Read the newspaper to identify and record any racist, violent acts. Discuss them with your family—their causes and the action you will take to prevent this from occurring to your family and to your community.
- Strive to eliminate racist language from your family's vocabulary. (Ford, 1994)

Step 2: Get to know someone different. As you continue your quest to learn more about your cultural heritage, learn about other racial and ethnic groups' heritages.

In one small, segregated Southern town, two business women—one African American and one White—decided it was time to bring "two worlds together." They organized two successful community potluck Sunday dinners at the local community college. For the first time in this community's history, African Americans and Whites ate dinner, talked, and played games together. Since everyone enjoyed these dinners, others are planned for the near future.

Other suggestions include the following:

- Make friends with someone from a different racial/ethnic group. Involve your children in this endeavor.
- Eat lunch with someone different. Invite him or her to a social event or go to an event together. Next, invite that person to your home for dinner. Make it a potluck, if you are unsure what to serve.
- Attend community multiethnic events such as cultural festivals, programs, and concerts.
- Organize ecumenical services to promote racial harmony.
- Volunteer at a multiethnic school to get exposure to different racial/ethnic groups.
- Attend your child's school and assess how racial harmony is promoted, and observe or ask whether the school's curriculum is culturally sensitive and diverse. Visit the school's library to determine whether multiethnic and culturally sensitive books, magazines, and other materials are available. If not, go to the school and advocate for the school system to purchase such books.

Step 3: Enrich your cultural experiences. To increase your knowledge base and skills regarding racism and cultural diversity, attend workshops, conferences, and meetings at your local colleges, universities, schools, churches, synagogues, temples, and/or libraries. Many organizations sponsor culturally related activities, such as ethnic food and music festivals. An excellent resource for increasing the family's knowledge base on race is the U.S. government's Information Agency's Web site titles "Perspectives on Race Relations in the U.S." It includes President Clinton's advisory board's report on race, a bibliography, and links to other Web sites addressing racial issues (United States Information Agency, 1998). Contact your local chamber of commerce or your local ethnic chamber, if available (e.g., the Asian Chamber of Commerce), for further information. Visit museums that celebrate diversity in person and/or via the World Wide Web. Carefully examine these museums to see how adequately cultures are represented. Some have excellent Web sites. Some examples include American Indian Centers, Inter-Tribal Cultural Centers; the Delta Cultural Center, a regional museum celebrating the richness of the Arkansas Delta; the Holocaust Museum, in Washington, D.C., which documents events of the Holocaust and is a memorial to those who lost their lives during that time; or the National Civil Rights Museum, located in Memphis, Tennessee, which documents the events of the Civil Rights Movement and the life of Dr. Martin Luther King. Be adventurous and take courses in ethnic or language studies offered at most colleges and universities.

Step 4: Become ambassadors for multi-ethnic diversity. Volunteer at schools, or with civic and youth groups that promote racial harmony or celebrate cultural diversity. Serve on interagency, organizational, and school boards to learn how your family can best contribute to your community. Encourage your child's participation in multiethnic organizations such as Girls Scouts, Boys Club, and the 4-H Clubs. Currently, the 4-H Club implements a curriculum, "Many Faces, One People," to teach children how to promote racial harmony and tolerance (Ruenzel, 1997).

Step 5: It all begins at home. Assess your home environment to make sure that it promotes and celebrates your family's racial and ethnic cultural heritage. Also, make sure it is free from stereotypical and racist pictures and artifacts. Expose your children to games, toys, and reading materials, etc., that reflect your identity, as well as that of others, in positive ways.

What's Happening on the Interpersonal Level with the Gomez Family?

"Informing and Influencing Others." We try to do our part to promote racial understanding and harmony. Together, Greg and I continue to do cultural sensitivity and awareness presentations for a myriad of groups, including schools and service organizations. As a board member for National Girl Scouts of America, my husband helps bring about greater awareness, understanding, and resources related to American Indian people. I share my experiences and expertise with college students, teaching them about their roles and responsibilities as future teachers of ethnically and culturally diverse students. Both Dulce and Golden Eagle make presentations in their classrooms and are learning to speak out for equity and justice in their school settings.

Third Level: Political Empowerment "We Shall Overcome"

This is the last level of the Empowerment Approach. At this level, the family is evolving in its role as an advocate against racism (alone or with others).

Voting is a powerful tool to eradicate racism. If members of your family are not registered to vote, contact your local voting registration office or your state's attorney general's office for information on where and how to register. The new Voters' Registration Law has made it easier to register.

Become more acquainted with your local, state, and national governments and how their electoral systems work. If possible, take a government class at your local college or university, or check the Internet for additional information and resources. Become an advocate for your family and community by attending meetings of the school board, the Parent Teachers Association, or your city council.

Organize a support group, such as a "Study Circle" (Ruenzel, 1997). A study circle is a "democratic tool" analogous to the town meeting, where individuals talk openly about their racial experiences and feelings within guidelines set by the group. A leader facilitates the discussion by asking questions and encouraging others to speak, but does not infringe his or her beliefs on the circle participants (Ruenzel, 1997).

Become familiar with laws (on all governmental levels) designed to protect American citizens' rights. Write letters, sign petitions, and speak out against any legislation that is not inclusive. In addition, speak out against insensitive printed or visual materials.

Become a member of national organizations that fight racism, such as the Southern Poverty Law Center, based in Montgomery, Alabama; the National Association for the Advancement of Colored People, in Baltimore, Maryland; and/or the National Alliance Against Racist and Political Repression, in New York (Ford, 1994).

What's Happening on the Political Level With the Gomez Family?

"We Shall Overcome." My family continuously advocates for diversity, equity, and justice; specifically, we do so on American Indian issues by writing letters, signing petitions, or supporting particular causes. For example, when we learned of some unsuccessful attempts to educate a university president and others regarding the stereotypical use of Indian mascots at their alma mater, we took action. Greg and I wrote letters to the university president and started a telephone and letter-writing campaign to engage other advocates. We also have signed petitions for the recognition and protection of sacred American Indian burial sites. Whenever possible, my family volunteers to support special causes such as the "1996 Peace Run," which went all the way to Mexico! My family believes that we have reached an even greater consciousness and sense of responsibility for making a difference, however small it may be.

Evaluation

Parents, you and your children are responsible for assessing your progress at each level. Remember, this is an ongoing process and a lifetime commitment. When you reach a level of frustration, step away and do something to reenergize your family— go to the movies, rent a video, or go for a walk in your neighborhood. Just continue your quest for empowerment. Some sample evaluation questions follow:

Personal: Am I using more positive, instead of negative, reinforcement? Are we praising and supporting each other?

Interpersonal: Have we established relationships with people from different racial/ethnic groups? Have we supported and/or attended a community event sponsored by another racial/ethnic group?

Political: Are eligible family members registered to vote? Have we joined organizations to combat racism?

As you progress, remember to update your Family Vision Statement. Set new goals, objectives, and timelines to include an action plan to end racism. Once empowered, you are a stronger advocate working to affect change and rid our society of racism.

Summary

Healing racism on a continuous basis is a lifetime commitment. The authors remain vigilant in their efforts to eradicate racism and promote racial harmony and solidarity forever. We strive to incorporate the levels and strategies presented in our Multidimensional Empowerment Approach by appreciating and respecting ourselves and others, keeping abreast of current information affecting diversity issues, and advocating for social change—whenever and wherever we go. Also, most important, we urge others to join the movement to promote racial unity for the next millennium. We hope our stories and approaches to heal racism will "spark" readers to follow the empowerment approaches to eradicate racism. Since it "takes a whole village" to free America of racism, remember to partner with your local communities, schools, religious institutions, and the government.

References

Angelou, M. (1994). *Phenomenal woman: Four poems celebrating women.* New York: Random House.

Barbour, C., & Barbour, N. H. (1997). *Families, schools, and communities: Building partnerships for educating children.* New Jersey: Prentice-Hall.

Barclay, K., & Boone, E. (1995). *Building a three way partnership: The leader's role in linking school, families and community.* New York: Scholastic.

Bell, D. (1992). *Faces at the bottom of the well: The permanence of racism.* New York: HarperCollins.

Blacks at the inaugural. (1997, March). *Ebony Magazine, 211*(5), 126-134.

Derman-Sparks, L., & ABC Task Force. (1989). *Anti-bias curriculum: Tools for empowering young children.* Washington, DC: National Association for the Education of Young Children.

Duvall, L. (1994). *Respecting our differences: A guide to getting along in a changing world.* Minneapolis, MN: Free Spirit Publishing.

Dyson, M. E. (1996). *Race rules: Navigating the color line.* Reading, MA: Addison-Wesley.

Ellerbee, L. (1992). *Nick news.* Nickelodeon.

Fletcher, M. A. (1998). President accepts report on race. *Washington Post* (On-line). Available: www.washingtonpost.com/wp-srv/national/longterm/race/race.

Ford, C. W. (1994). *We can all get along.* New York: Doubleday Dell.

Franklin, J. H., & Moss, A. A., Jr. (1980). *From slavery to freedom* (6th ed.). New York: Alfred A. Knopf.

Gestwicki, C. (1996). *Home, school, and community relations: A guide to working with parents* (3rd ed.). Albany, NY: Delmar.

Gutierrez, L. M. (1994-95, Fall/Winter). *Empowerment and Latinos: Implications for practice* (Volume 13, Numbers III & IV). Chicago, IL: Family Resource Coalition.

Holman, C. (1994, February). Tapestry: The common threads of human diversity in America. *Dallas Morning News,* p. 12.

Hopson, D. P., & Hopson, D. S. (1990). *Different and wonderful: Raising black children in a race-conscious society.* New York: Fireside.

Hopson, D. P., Hopson, D. S., & Clavin, T. (1993). *Raising the rainbow generation: Teaching your children to be successful in a multicultural society.* New York: Fireside.

Leland, J., & Samuels, A. (1997). The new generation gap. *Newsweek, 129,* pp. 52-60.

Lyon, G. (1997, Spring). Unite and overcome! *Teaching Tolerance, 6*(1), 11-15.

Mathias, B., & French, M. (1996). *40 ways to raise a nonracist child.* New York: HarperCollins.

Mfume, K. (1997). Personal communication with Phyllis Hammonds.

Ruenzel, D. (1997, Spring). Crucial conversations. *Teaching Tolerance, 6*(1), 19-23.

Sleeter, C. E. (1992). *Keepers of the American dream: A study of staff development and multicultural education.* Washington, DC: Falmer Press.

Steinem, G. (1992). *Revolution from within: A book of self-esteem.* New York: Little, Brown.

U.S. Department of Health and Human Services. (1998). *Family partnerships: A continuous process. Training guides for the Head Start learning community* (National Alliance of Business contract no. 105-93-1586). Washington, DC: Author.

U.S. Information Agency. (1998). *Perspectives on race relations in the U.S.* (on-line). Author. Available: www.gov./usa/race.

White House names advisory board on race. (1997, June 13). *USA Today,* p. 4a.

chapter V

Dealing With Issues of Racism in the Classroom: Preservice and Beginning Teachers

Norvella P. Carter, *Texas A&M University*
Anne Gayles-Felton, *Florida A&M University*
Robert Hilliard, *State University of West Georgia*
Larry A. Vold, *Indiana University of Pennsylvania*

Mark Twain reportedly once said that "everybody talks about the weather, but nobody does anything about it." Perhaps much the same could be said about racism. Like the weather, it's with us every day, but also like the weather, most people neglect to read the signs of potential storms that are brewing within the social context of our daily lives. You can't pick up a newspaper or turn on a television without finding some reference to America's ongoing malady: racism.

A 4-year-old's voice pierces the calm on a beautiful, warm afternoon at a neighborhood pool: "I don't like Black people at my pool." Her mother is mortified for several reasons, including the fact that child clearly intended to be heard by the Black couple a few feet away. A 5-year-old in a grocery store says, nonchalantly, "Daddy, why do that lady's eyes go up like this?," and then pulls the corners of his eyes up in a slant (Dupecher, 1994). Dupecher states that these and similar incidents are familiar to anyone who spends time around young children. Early in life, children learn and imitate prejudice. Unless they learn to accept and appreciate differences among people, they will innocently pattern prejudicial behavior. Often, those prejudicial patterns and behaviors are first learned from parents.

Our population is becoming increasingly diverse, and the future belongs to the leaders of business, industry, and culture who can best relate to racial diversity. It is clear that children must be taught tolerance and appreciation not only of racial differences, but also of differences of any kind, including gender, disability, ethnicity, religion, or social class (Dupecher, 1994). Unfortunately, the nation's universities and colleges rarely send new teachers into the educational arena with a solid framework for dealing with racism as it occurs in the classroom (Grant & Sleeter, 1986; Sleeter, 1992).

The purpose of this chapter is to provide preservice and beginning teachers with some insight by discussing the issue of racism, as set forth in four parts. First, we will discuss the demographics, preparation, and responsibility associated with racism. Second, we will examine the role of the teacher's belief system in addressing racism in the classroom. Third, we will review anecdotes of incidents with racial overtones experienced by college supervisors, preservice teachers, and experienced teachers. Finally, we will make recommendations to preservice and beginning teachers for responding to racial incidents, with a special emphasis on implications for teacher educators.

Demographics, Preparation, and Responsibility for Dealing with Racism

To begin any discussion of racism, it is important to look at the overall composition of the nation's teachers. Traditionally, teachers in the United States have been White, female, and from working-class or middle-class cultures (American Association of Colleges for Teacher Education, 1990; Apple, 1986; Banks, 1991; Goodlad, 1991; National Education Association, 1996). The student population, however, is much more diverse than that. Approximately 88 percent of the teaching force is White, yet African American, Native American, Hispanic, and Asian children constitute nearly 40 percent of the public school population (National Center for Education Statistics, 1992).

Teachers from White, working-class, or middle-class cultures often are not prepared to deal with racism in the classroom, and so they tend to avoid the subject. In fact, for the majority of these teachers, racism is not easy to acknowledge or confront (Benton & Daniel, 1996). White teacher education students often distance themselves from racism (Sleeter, 1992; Tatum, 1992). In Wellman's (1993) case studies, he found that the White women and men he interviewed tended to believe that racism was synonymous with personal prejudice; because they did not feel prejudiced, they believed that racism must be someone else's problem.

According to Menz (1996), Whites' avoidance of race issues can be attributed to "a kind of artificial colorblindness" that is used to manage "discomfort and the possibility of conflict around racial differences" (p. 245). Valli (1995) discusses the conflict between these popular sayings: "If you don't see color, you don't see the child" and "Teachers should be colorblind" (p. 121). Teachers who do not "see" color are prone to imposing a Eurocentric, White culture on children of color. Consequently, they fail to acknowledge and meet those children's needs. In this sense, teachers need to see color. Conversely, color should cease to matter if it is being used as a barrier. If recognition of color causes low expectations, hostility, or other negative reactions, then color must become invisible. Valli (1995) refers to this as "America's schizophrenia about racial color" (p. 121). Teachers must see color and not see color at the same time. Furthermore, the colorblind model is grounded in the view that it is not polite to talk about race (Boutte, LaPoint, & Davis, 1993). Although Greene (1995) points out the value in raising the issue of race, it is seldom discussed in classrooms. According to Fine (1993), students quickly find out that racism, discrimination, and other "dangerous" topics are not supposed to be discussed in school.

Tatum (1992) explains three major reasons why students are resistant to talking and learning about race and racism:

- Race is considered a taboo topic for discussion, especially in racially mixed settings
- Many students, regardless of race, have been socialized to think of the United States as a just society

- Many students, particularly White students, initially deny any personal prejudice; they recognize the impact of racism on other people's lives, but fail to acknowledge its impact on their own. (p. 5)

Tatum's work reveals that students are resistant to developing a knowledge base or strategies for dealing with racism. It follows, then, that preservice and beginning teachers, as a whole, have trouble identifying or resolving racial incidents. This difficulty stems from the fact that they have very little preparation for doing so.

Regardless of the circumstances, teachers have a moral responsibility and obligation to deal with racism in the classroom. According to Lasley and Biddle (1996), many teachers believe they do not have the right to communicate values and character education to young people. The U.S. Supreme Court, however, stated explicitly that teachers have the responsibility to inculcate "the shared values of a civilized social order" (*Bethel School District No. 403 v. Fraser*, 1986). The literature reveals overwhelming support for a set of core values, including the confrontation of racism. These core values are shared by most Americans, including those social and cultural groups currently represented in public schools in the United States (Bennett, 1995; Gay, 1994; Irvine, 1994; Lickona, 1988; Scott, 1995; Steller & Lambert, 1996; Tierno, 1996).

Teachers are role models as well as transmitters of values; as such, they must not hesitate to teach character whenever moral questions arise (Damon, 1988). Value-free classrooms do not exist; in fact, the question is not *whether* schools should teach values, but *how* to teach such qualities as honesty, courage, fairness, justice, and responsibility (Cline & Necochea, 1996). Scott (1995) believes that teachers who were reared and socialized in White cultures and educated at predominantly White institutions must examine their own prejudices and stereotypes about ethnic minorities before they can combat racism and become effective in multicultural classrooms. In addition, Scott (1995) asserts that teacher educators must accept the obligation and responsibility to facilitate experiences, discussions, and feedback for preservice teachers and help them to interpret their perceptions about minority related issues.

Preservice and inservice teachers should "develop a commitment to combat racism and all forms of prejudice and discrimination through the development of appropriate understanding, attitudes and social action skills" (Bennett, 1995, p. 263). Specifically:

- There should be an emphasis on clearing up racial myths and stereotypes about the inferiority of different races and cultures, as well as an emphasis on stressing basic human similarities and connections
- There should be an awareness of the origins, persistence, and impact of institutional and cultural racism in the United States and elsewhere in the world
- Once there is a recognition of the realities of racism, teachers should strive to become antiracist
- Antiracist teachers will create equitable classroom environments, characterized by high achievement expectations for all students and coupled with culturally and linguistically appropriate teaching strategies and assessments
- Antiracist teachers will create an antiracist curriculum that goes beyond cultural celebrations to embracing decision-making and social action. (pp. 263-264)

Teachers' daily decisions, including those related to curricular choices, also affect students' character development. Haberman and Post (1992) stress the view that preservice teachers need to have frequent dialogue and feedback with sensitive and knowledgeable faculty. They need to talk about what they are seeing, feeling, and experiencing with minority students, as well as with minorities in general. Haberman and Post (1992) believe that stereotypes and prejudices will be reinforced if this intervention and sensitization does not occur. Given the important role that educational experiences have in shaping and molding a student's character, teachers must prepare themselves to address the issue of race and racism, and they need to actively participate in students' character formation.

No matter the level of discomfort in talking about race, preservice teachers need training in this area. Carter and Larke (1995) reported findings that showed some preservice students could find no fault with simply not wanting to teach certain types of children, based on their race and socioeconomic factors. The authors of this chapter are especially disturbed by a study (McDiarmid & Price, 1993) that found that preservice teachers persisted in making decisions based on stereotypes, despite taking part in a three-day workshop about important content for working with African Americans, Hispanics, Native Americans, and Asians. Law and Lane (1987) found that preservice teachers in the United States often have negative views about minority cultural groups. John Goodlad (1991) reported that some education majors did not believe that all students could learn. In addition, at the university level, classes are not consistently offered on the subject of racism, and some studies emphasize that talking about race and learning about racism is difficult for students in general (Cochran-Smith, 1995; Tatum, 1992; Valli, 1995). Cochran-Smith (1995) reported that many of her preservice teachers admitted having uncertainty about discussing race-related issues, especially in racially mixed groups. Her preservice teachers asked the following questions: How do we help children develop their own racial and cultural identities and establish meaningful relationships with children of other races and cultures when we ourselves are uncomfortable with that? And do we help children when, in fact, we have failed for most of our adult lives to talk directly

> **How do we help children develop their own racial and cultural identities and establish meaningful relationships with children of other races and cultures when we ourselves are uncomfortable with that?**

and constructively with others about issues of race and culture (p. 558)?

Preservice teachers are not the only ones expressing doubts about these issues. Solomon (1995) reported that even veteran teachers lack training in multicultural and anti-racist education. She reported these viewpoints:

(Teacher #1)   I don't feel prepared to deal with racism as a topic in the classroom, or as prepared as I feel I should be. I'm very concerned about hurting students' feelings indirectly when trying to deal with racist attitudes.

(Teacher #2)   Some members of our staff are afraid of teaching multicultural and anti-racist education that may insult some parents. I believe that guidelines and suggestions on what to teach will encourage some teachers to make it a part of their program. (p. 253)

Solomon (1995) indicated that teachers resisted focusing on the area of race specifically because they did not perceive racism to be a problem in their schools. Various other studies support the view that teachers avoid issues that revolve around racism (Benton, 1994; Benton & Daniel, 1996; Boyle, 1982; Grant & Sleeter, 1986; Rist, 1978; Sleeter, 1992).

Fortunately, some teacher education programs provide opportunities for learning about multicultural education (Gollnick, 1996; Grant & Tate, 1995; Ladson-Billings, 1994). Research suggests that anti-racist teacher education courses can help White students recognize racial oppression (Bollin & Finkel, 1995; McCall, 1995) and help them gain insight into their Whiteness and what it means (Lawrence, 1997; Lawrence & Bunche, 1996; Tatum, 1992; Valli, 1995). We hope that our presentation of anecdotal incidents may provide preservice teachers with personal and professional insights, while also helping them to change their attitudes and convictions.

The Role of the Teacher's Belief System in the Classroom

Prospective and beginning teachers must have a strong, accurate knowledge base and belief system on the issue of racism. Beliefs are representations of the information a person has about another person, group of people, place, or thing; they may be based on fact or on opinion (Mueller, 1986). Rokeach (1968) defined a belief system ". . . as having represented within it, in some organized psychological but not necessarily logical form, each and every one of a person's countless beliefs about physical and social reality" (p. 2). The information and knowledge that teachers acquire shape their beliefs, behavior, and decisions in the classroom.

The things that teachers say, perceive, believe, and think can disable or empower students (Nel, 1993). Pajares (1992) expresses the view

. . . that the beliefs teachers hold influence their perceptions and judgments, which in turn, affect their behavior in the classroom, or that understanding the belief structures of teachers and teacher candidates is essential to improving their professional preparation and teaching practices. (p. 307)

young to understand the messages of tolerance: trust, respect, fairness?" (p. 10). School-age children are not too young to engage in discussions about racial issues. Perhaps the incident just cited would not have occurred if the teacher had been proactive in her discussions about race. Even if race issues had been previously reviewed, this incident would have been an ideal opportunity for additional discussion.

Incidents #2 and #3. A kindergarten teacher reported the following two incidents. In her first year, an African American child came running to her on the playground with a small cut on his forehead. He claimed that another child, a White boy, had thrown a rock at him. Seeing this as a behavioral problem and not as a racial incident, she attended to the cut and then asked the offending boy to apologize and explain his actions. He told her calmly that they, meaning he and the other White boys, didn't want the Black boy to play with them and he threw the rock to make him go away. The incident was reported to the principal as required by the district, but it was not treated as a racial incident. This teacher's standard kindergarten lessons on "same" and "different" took on a new meaning. She was able to respond proactively because the stage had been set for teaching respect for others.

Some years later, two girls (one African American, the other White) each came to school wearing the same new dress. It did not go unnoticed, as a young White boy blurted out, "Look, Tamika and Shelley look like twins! Except that" (and the teacher cringed, expecting the worst and knowing that she could not stop the child from saying what he was about to say) ". . . except that Shelley has a ribbon in her hair." The previous day's lessons on "same" and "different" had not been lost on him. The teacher seized the moment and spent a good part of that morning and the rest of the week discussing differences and similarities, a discussion that included not only issues of racial similarities and differences, but also those of gender and diversity.

Dupecher (1994) states that schooling children in differences is at the heart of raising them to be bias-free.

A group of preschoolers, each holding a lemon, is seated in a circle on the floor. "This is your lemon," the teacher says. "Get to know it." The children inspect their lemons carefully. They roll them, throw them up in the air, twirl them on end, and finger every dent and imperfection. "Now, put your lemon in this paper bag," the teacher directs. Challenged minutes later to "find your lemon," [each] preschooler succeeds. "Mine was a darker yellow," one student points out, while another one notes, "Mine had a bump on the side." "You are like your lemon," the teacher explains. "Each of you is different." She then collects the lemons and later returns them to the children— peeled. "But I can't find mine! They all look the same!" the children exclaim. The children learn a vital lesson in being different on the outside, but alike on the inside. (Dupecher, 1994, p. 23)

Children are aware of differences very early in their development. In fact, this ability to discriminate, and the bias that may result, represents a natural phase in early childhood development, according to Lilian G. Katz, a professor of early childhood education at the University of Illinois at Urbana-Champaign.

"Every child goes through a time when he or she says, 'My way is right. The way my family eats breakfast is right. The way I dress is right,' " Katz says (Dupecher, 1994, p. 4). "It's natural for children to notice differences, and psychologically healthy for them

at a young age to value their way of doing things. The problem is to outgrow that."
Katz adds that noticing racial differences occurs in three stages. Around ages 2 1/2 to
3, preschoolers become aware of physical differences such as skin color, facial features,
and hair type. In the next stage, when children acquire the language to describe and
define racial groups, they are likely to pick up the feelings and attitudes of the significant
others around them. In the final stage, children begin to understand the permanence of
characteristics such as skin, hair, and eye color. During this period, children may tend
to overgeneralize, believing, for example, that all women with gray hair are grandmoth-
ers. Stereotyping begins. Stereotyping is not, however, limited to the very young.

To further understand living with stereotypes, John Ogbu (1992) classified minority
groups as 1) immigrant or voluntary minorities, and 2) castelike or involuntary
minorities. Minorities in the first category have moved voluntarily, more or less, to
the United States because they desire economic well-being, better overall opportunities, and/or greater political freedom. Involuntary minorities were originally brought
into the United States against their will through slavery, conquest, colonization, or
forced labor. Such minorities often were relegated to menial positions and denied
true assimilation into the mainstream society. This group is more likely to experience
greater and more persistent difficulties with school learning.

Is racism, then, a clash not of race necessarily, but rather of culture and the bond
(or lack) of common experiences? Belonging is an interesting concept and may tran-
scend racial prejudices as we seek to understand some racial "incidents." A teacher
in Arkansas says that students, Black and White, who were reared together since
kindergarten, have begun picking on the Hispanics who have begun to move into the
district in increasing numbers. Another teacher reports that first-generation Mexican
Americans, whose parents were born in Mexico, have little to do with age-mates who
were born in Mexico and only recently immigrated to the United States. Yet another
teacher notes that his African American and Caucasian students were more likely to
present a solid front against the Hispanic (primarily Mexican) students who were new
to the community. In this instance, the students were more likely to form alliances
with those they had known since early childhood, whatever the race.

Incident #4. A fight between a 3rd-grade Hispanic boy and an African American classmate was
immediately treated as a racial incident by many, including the teacher, until a parent conference was called. In the conference, it became evident that both boys had been taught by their
fathers to learn to "stand up for themselves," and if that involved fighting, they were told not to
hesitate. Both fathers claimed no racial animosity and the boys had not reverted to any name
calling as a part of the fight.

We chose to include Incident #4 to demonstrate an important point. Many incidents
that could appear to be racial may actually not be. We must be careful that in our rush
to eradicate racism, we don't create an even larger incident. While we should not fear
to address incidents if they are racially motivated, we should attend to the behavior first.

What is the best way to respond when people who have experienced overt racism begin
seeing racial motivations in any experience that contradicts their personal belief system? A
college supervisor, for example, reports an incident in which a Caucasian teacher had

trouble communicating constructive criticism to an African American student teacher. The teacher carefully documented the student teacher's tardies, unexplained absences, failure to prepare lessons, and inability to obtain materials for teaching. The teacher, with the college supervisor and building principal, attempted to conference and remediate, but the student saw only racial motivations and would not change. When the student teacher was pulled from her assignment, she sued.

Life does not come with easy answers. Life is not always fair. But do we make it even more difficult to heal racial prejudices when we aggravate racial tensions? Perhaps we need to face up to our own prejudices, which are largely a matter of our own, often limited, life experiences. We need to seek the best in each other without attributing differences to racial motivations. We need to seek to know each other better, and to teach tolerance, respect, and responsibility for one's own actions. We need to recognize that each of us, of any race, represents our race to others.

Incident #5. A preschool teacher shared an incident in which two African American 4-year-old boys were arguing. One called the other a n——-, to which the child, an African American albino, replied, "I'm not a n——-, I'm White," and walked away. Having used the High-Scope program, the teacher had taught children to work through confrontations on their own (without adult interference). While continuing to work with other children, she kept one eye on the situation. Moments later, the two boys were playing together. She said nothing to them at the time. The High-Scope program, which is used by many schools, does appear to help children learn to address confrontation and make good decisions.

One of the authors recalls an attempt to avoid cultural clashes while employed as a school district administrator. Students at one of the high schools sponsored a multicultural day, inviting several speakers, including Native Americans, African Americans, Africans, Vietnamese, and others from the community and local state college. The students at the school often segregated themselves by race. Through guided discussions during the multicultural day, students noted that recent immigrants often grouped themselves by language because they were more comfortable speaking their own language. A student from South America spent more time with Vietnamese students because he was more comfortable with others who were "new" even if they were from a different culture. Most of the White students had known each other since kindergarten, had grown up in the same neighborhoods, and therefore believed they had no need to acquire new friends. They weren't "anti-" anyone. They weren't overly racist, in their view; they were just comfortable with their own cliques and hadn't considered including others. Students who had little to say to or do with Native American students listened closely to Native American speakers and, for the first time, were guided into conversations with fellow students of all representative cultures. Lack of mutual experiences and different interests were obstacles.

Again, much of what could have been taken as racism was more a matter of accepting those with whom we've grown up, those we know and understand. Perhaps that becomes an important message in approaching racism from a healing perspective. Put it into perspective. Address the behaviors. Understand the social implications as well as the maturity and life experiences of the respondents. Southerners are often "fussing" about Northerners' accents, customs, attitudes, even their food and music preferences, for example. People of color and Caucasians alike enjoy the barbeque style that is favored in their local area. Even in the South, disagreements occur on what is the best way to barbecue. What may, at first glance, appear to be racist behaviors may only reflect a higher comfort level with one's local customs and experiences.

One male professor who was born in Africa to an American (Cherokee) mother and an African father had an interesting experience. At the historically African American institution where he taught, he was often ostracized by African American colleagues born in the United States. The professor now reports that he experiences hardly any racial prejudice at the predominantly Caucasian institution where he currently teaches. In fact, he is included in personal, social, and professional activities. In the first institution, he was regularly exposed to overt racism by "educated" colleagues. The authors include this anecdote to point out that racism is not necessarily a matter of race versus race, or White versus people of color.

Incident #6. A student teacher had been teaching the concepts of symbolism and patriotism to her 3rd-graders. She had shown pictures and used materials depicting the Liberty Bell, the Statue of Liberty, the American flag, and other symbols. She had discussed the meaning of symbols and the concept of patriotism before asking the students to create their own symbol of what "America means to me." While students were busy drawing and coloring, the student teacher walked around the room monitoring and assisting. One girl was drawing an outline of the United States and had placed in the center (from coast to coast) faces of children representing a multicultural mix of races. Her drawing was titled "America is a family." A young boy was busy with his drawing of the state flag, which includes the Confederate stars and bars. The teacher asked the boy if he was familiar with the controversy surrounding the state flag (because of the Confederate elements), hoping to make the point that perhaps his drawing represented, at best, an inappropriate symbol, one that, moreover, applied only to one state. As she was talking and listening, the young man made the comment, "You know, if we'd won that war, some of those people [Black students] would be working for me and you." Although not prepared for such a remark, and believing that the remark was not heard by other students, the teacher took the opportunity with the entire class to display several drawings (including the "America is a family" drawing) and to discuss what a family means and how we got to be a family. She discussed immigration, slave trade, injustice, prejudice, and tolerance, but she was not satisfied that she had made a difference. While she did not confront the flag-drawing student directly, she continued to look for ways to include multicultural concepts in her teaching.

Wayson (1988) surveyed student teachers at Ohio State University and found them to have negative attitudes or to be ill-informed on issues dealing with minority student problems. Less than half believed that achievement might improve if preservice teachers took courses dealing with racism. Wayson (1988) also discovered that four-fifths of the students did not believe that the issue of race needed to be dealt with in order to establish a positive learning environment in the classroom.

Incident #7. A 2nd-grader asked that she no longer be called Valencia, but wanted instead to be called Jennifer. Concerned, the teacher called the child's grandmother to discuss the name change and to solicit advice. After a telephone call and a visit to the classroom, the grandmother gave the teacher permission to begin calling the child Jennifer. Although it was against the teacher's best judgment, the child, who was academically and socially behind most of her classmates, became "Jennifer." Almost immediately, her grades and social behaviors improved. While disturbed by the notion that the child might see herself as somehow inferior (as an African American), the teacher and grandmother hoped that with social and academic improvement, the child's self-image might improve to the point that she would once again be comfortable being Valencia.

Racism is a societal creature, and young children often succumb to feelings they do not understand. The teacher, while admitting to not understanding all the racial dynamics that exist in the classroom (to her credit), was already very sensitive to individual feelings and worked each day to build social and academic confidence in each child. This incident shows a teacher who wants to be sensitive and meet the needs of her students. It also reveals, however, a teacher who is using the deficit model. The teacher makes the assumption that the child wants a name change because she feels inferior and has a problem with self-image. One operating from the deficit model would say that Valencia probably does not like being Black and wants to shed everything associated with it.

If one views this incident outside of the deficit model, one would say that Valencia does not feel inferior, nor does she have a problem with self-image. She was learning how to negotiate the system so that it works for her. Apparently, Valencia observed a "Jennifer" or a "Jennifer-type" who had what she wanted, in terms of teacher responses and behavior. By taking on a name that represented more attention from the teacher, she received acceptance and better treatment by all.

In these and other incidents, teachers may want to simply ask the students what is happening and let them explain their behaviors, rather than indulging in a guessing game. African American children, in general, are very person-to-person oriented in terms of their learning style (Larke, Webb-Johnson, & Carter, 1996). Students need to develop personal relationships with their teachers. Teachers should take an interest in what their students are doing and feeling. They should also take time to interact with family members. This person-to-person style can help teachers be more effective, both in and out of the classroom. The "name change" incident, for example, caused the teacher to get much more involved in her student's life.

Incident #8. A White high school teacher participated in a race relations workshop presented by the Anti-Defamation League, and decided to engage his students, all White, in one of the activities. The activity was called "Name Five," and required the students to write the names of 5 prominent Americans on a sheet of paper in one minute. The person could be living or dead, but they had to be "real" as opposed to fictional people. "Prominent" was defined as any American who would be recognized by the entire class. The students wrote the first set of names in a manner of seconds. The activity continued as follows:

Write the names of 5 prominent African Americans.
Write the names of 5 prominent Hispanic Americans.
Write the names of 5 prominent Asian Americans.
Write the names of 5 prominent Native Americans.

When asked how they fared in completing the activity, all had completed the names of prominent Americans and prominent African Americans. None of the 27 students could write five names for each of the last three categories. Students were asked why they could not write names of Hispanic, Asian, and Native Americans. Some of their responses were:

I needed more time.

I never thought about it before.

I just couldn't think that fast.

I never learned about them in school.

I couldn't do it because I don't pay attention to color; people are people.

This community is White, the school is White; we don't focus on other people.

When asked how they felt about the activity, some of the responses were:

This was a great activity.

I'm going to do this with my family.

Why do we have to do this?

It really made me think.

I don't think this was fair.

I felt stupid.

I felt ignorant.

I was shocked that I could not do it.

Although surprised that some of the students seemed upset by the activity, the teacher explained that this activity was not a reflection of their intelligence, but rather a reflection of their schooling; therefore, they should not feel "stupid." The teacher also explained that all students should know about the contributions of all the cultures in the United States.

This teacher was operating from a position that fits into the model of multicultural education. He engaged his students in a simple activity that enabled them to see the need for a more comprehensive knowledge base. One of the goals of multicultural education is to assist all students, including White students, to develop the knowledge, skills, and attitudes that are necessary to live and work effectively in U.S. society, a society in which soon one out of every three people will be a person of color (Banks, 1994). White students will be imperiled if they do not attain the knowledge and skills needed to live in a culturally pluralistic society. It is important for them to understand and recognize that all students benefit from a multicultural education.

Incident #9. A White, first-year teacher in a predominantly White setting listened as a 10th-grade Native American student shared his disdain for the Indian mascot that had been the school mascot for 40 years. Initially, the teacher wondered why this would bother him. The mascot plays a major role in school festivities. The teacher never really thought about the giant, scantily dressed mascot that stands in a glass case in the school lobby. After the student's comments, however, the teacher found herself bothered by the mascot. She did not mention her feelings about it to anyone, but did ask the principal if anyone ever challenged the mascot. His response was "Are you kidding, everyone loves our mascot." Nothing more has been said.

Apparently, the Native American student had an impact on the heart and mind of this teacher, but she more or less avoided the issue. Hopefully, this teacher will get to know the student better and learn more about his feelings and perceptions. It is difficult to find large numbers of studies that deal with Native American students' perceptions (one that does was conducted by Pewewardy and Willower, 1993). During the 1990s, Native Americans protested against their image being used as mascots on college and professional sports teams, as well as against other American traditions that are offensive to Native Americans. Shutiva (1995), a Native American, discusses racism and writes the following about mascots:

Although each tribe is distinctly different from the other, the diversity, esteem and sovereignty of each tribe is negated by the sweeping terms, Redskins, Braves and Indians. Being the mascot of a sports team is not deemed as an honor or a privilege. Instead, these names promote a stereotypical image that Native Americans are savage, aggressive, ruthless and cunning, akin to creatures of the animal kingdom (i.e., cougars, bears, tigers and lions, which are also mascot names of sports teams). (p. 72)

The spiritual elements important to Native Americans also are being exploited, commercialized, and distorted. These issues are not often discussed in classrooms, although the majority of Native American students attend public schools (Bureau of Indian Affairs, 1988).

Incident #10. A student teacher was transferred from one school setting into another. The supervising teacher had seen no problems and was completely surprised. A discussion with the Director of Field Experiences revealed that the student teacher was in a biracial marriage; her husband was an African American who worked with the community recreation program and as a referee in local athletic competitions. It seems that several students learned that the student teacher and the community worker were married, and it had become the topic of some conversation. It was not a topic of conversation among the faculty, many of whom knew both the husband and student teacher. The supervising teacher did not make a connection and had no concerns. The student teacher was transferred to a community where biracial marriages, although not common, do exist. The teacher subsequently called the student teacher to learn what she could do about the situation, and is still unaware of any problems between the student teacher and herself or any of her students. From what the supervising teacher is able to discover, it was more of an issue of comfort for the student teacher regarding her students. The supervising teacher is still unsure of what could have been said or done or even what should now be said or done.

A community in Georgia made the news ("Time To Bury Church's Racism," 1996) when a local church refused to let the child of a biracial couple be buried in the church cemetery. The woman had been reared in the church and the controversy divided the community. Opportunities to discuss issues of biracial marriages and other racial issues abound every day in local and national news reports. What does the student teacher say when confronted by students who want to know what they think?

Recommendations and Conclusions

Teachers are faced with the responsibility and challenge of educating children to become citizens of a democratic and pluralistic nation. Teachers who are committed to this task will not allow racism to hinder their efforts. A student's race is an intimate component of his or her self-esteem. How teachers react to this aspect of the student as a human being has a tremendous effect on social and academic achievement in the classroom. The manner in which racial issues are handled in the classroom determines if racism will be perpetuated or discouraged. Here are recommendations for preservice and new teachers who are beginning the battle against racism in schools. First, review what you learned in your multicultural education, racism, and diversity courses. If you have not taken courses in these areas, engage in professional development activities that will help you to become informed.

Second, examine yourself and know your biases. While everyone has biases, they can control their own classroom behavior. Teachers must model behaviors that indicate respect for individuals and groups, especially in situations that involve disagreement, regardless of personal biases. A teacher should always be caring and unprejudiced, and should not show racial and ethnic favoritism or practice racial exploitation.

Do not avoid issues of racism as they arise in your classroom. The only way to combat racism is to confront it immediately. In addition, you must have open, honest, yet non-offensive discussions about race with your students if you want a healthy and productive multicultural environment. In a class that is mixed racially and attitudinally, a teacher should try to discuss with students their fears and prejudices in an accepting and nonjudgmental manner. It is important for the lines of communication to always be open among parents, teachers, and learners. A teacher should encourage and respond to learners' spontaneous questions, comments, and concerns about race, in terms of the learners' maturity levels. Racist comments should be dealt with immediately, and in a straightforward manner.

You also must be willing to take a stand for what you believe is fair, equitable, and right. You are in a position that gives you the privilege of helping to build children's character. Take it seriously, and do not be afraid to share positions with the students that build integrity. A teacher's behavior should always demonstrate sincere sensitivity to the cultures and lifestyles of all the races and ethnicities represented by the class. Recognition of and respect for family members' attitudes and cherished values, when dealing with the emotional and personal aspects of race and racism, are essential.

At all costs, avoid engaging in the deficit model. The belief that some people are deficient in intelligence and/or achievement because of genetics or because of cultural background is detrimental to all children. Talk to other educators who have experience with diversity, and seek other perspectives to ensure that you are not unconsciously engaging in this model. A teacher in a multicultural classroom should plan frequent educational experiences that focus upon racial and ethnic differences and similarities, in order to help learners care about, and relate to, people of diverse backgrounds, cul-tures, and lifestyles. A teacher should plan specific curricular experiences to help learners acquire significant knowledges about other ethnic and racial groups. Understanding people and their cultures is basic to promoting good human relations.

Finally, teacher educators have the responsibility to pre-pare teachers to be optimally effective in educating all children for life in a pluralistic society. In addition, teacher education insti-tutions must face the challenge of providing veteran teachers with multi-cultural education through inservices and staff development opportunities. Teachers who desire to eradicate racism must be supported, trained, and encouraged.

References

Aaronsohn, E., Carter, C., & Howell, M. (1995). Preparing monocultural teachers for a multicultural world: Attitudes toward inner-city schools. *Equity & Excellence in Education, 28*(1), 5-9.

American Association of Colleges of Teacher Education. (1990). *Teacher education pipeline II: Schools, colleges and departments of education enrollments by race and ethnicity.* Washington, DC: Author.

Apple, M. (1986). *Teachers and texts.* New York: Routledge & Kegan Paul.

Banks, J. (1991). Teaching multicultural literacy to teachers. *Teacher Education, 4*(1), 135-144.

Banks, J. (1993). Multicultural education: Historical development, dimensions, and practice. In L. Darling-Hammond (Ed.), *Review of research in education,* Vol. 19 (pp. 3-49). Washington, DC: American Educational Research Association.

Banks, J. (1994). *An introduction to multicultural education.* Needham Heights, MA: Allyn and Bacon.

Bennett, C. (1995). Preparing teachers for cultural diversity and national standards of academic excellence. *Journal of Teacher Education, 46*(4), 259-295.

Bennett, G. K., et al. (1970). Response to Robert Williams. *The Counseling Psychologist, 2*(2), 88-96.

Benton, J. (1994). *Getting along, getting ahead: Three secondary English teachers' beliefs and practices in cultural diversity.* Unpublished doctoral dissertation, University of Georgia, Athens.

Benton, J., & Daniel, P. (1996). Learning to talk about taboo topics: A first step in examining cultural diversity with preservice teachers. *Equity & Excellence in Education, 29*(3), 8-17.

Bethel School District No. 403 v. Fraser, 675-96. (1986). United States Supreme Court Report.

Bollin, G. G., & Finkel, J. (1995). White racial identity as a barrier to understanding diversity: A study of preservice teachers. *Equity and Excellence in Education, 28*(1), 25-30.

Boutte, G., LaPoint, S., & Davis, B. (1993). Racial issues in education: Real or imagined? *Young Children, 48*(6), 19-22.

Boyle, M. (1982). Teaching in a desegregated and mainstreamed school: A study of the affirmation of human diversity (Doctoral dissertation, University of Wisconsin-Madison, 1982). *Dissertation Abstracts International, 43,* 2215A.

Bureau of Indian Affairs. (1988). *U.S. Department of the Interior budget justifications.* Washington, DC: U.S. Department of the Interior.

Carter, N., & Larke, P. (1995). Preparing the urban teacher: Reconceptualizing the experience. In M. O'Hair & S. Odell (Eds.), *Educating teachers for leadership and change: ATE yearbook* (pp. 77-95). Thousand Oaks, CA: Corwin Press.

Cline, Z., & Necochea, J. (1996). An effective character education model for a diverse student population. *The Education Forum, 60*(2), 165-173.

Cochran-Smith, M. (1995). Uncertain allies: Understanding the boundaries of race and teaching. *Harvard Educational Review, 65*(4), 541-570.

Damon, W. (1988). *The moral child: Nurturing children's natural moral growth.* New York: Free Press.

Dupecher, M. (1994). Breeding bigotry out of children. *Kiwanis, 48,* 2-4, 22-25.

Fine, M. (1993). "You can't just say that the only ones who can speak are those who agree with your position": Political discourse in the classroom. *Harvard Educational Review, 63*(1), 412-433.

Gay, G. (1994). *At the essence of learning. Multicultural education.* West Lafayette, IN: Kappa Delta Pi.

Gollnick, D. M. (1996). Can arts and sciences faculty prepare quality teachers? *American Behavioral Scientist, 40*(2), 233-241.

Goodlad, J. (1991). *Teacher for our nation's schools.* San Francisco: Jossey-Bass.

Grant, C., & Sleeter, C. (1986). *After the school bell rings.* London: Falmer Press.

Grant, C. A., & Tate, W. F. (1995). *Multicultural education through the lens of the multicultural education research literature.* ERIC Document ED 382704.

Greene, B. (1995). Addressing race, class, and gender in Zora Neale Hurston's "The Eyes Were Watching God": Strategies & reflections. *English Education, 27*(4), 268-276.

Haberman, M., & Post, L. (1992). Does direct experience change education students' perceptions of low-income minority children? *Mid-Western Education Researcher, 5*(2), 29-31.

Hilliard, R., & Vold, L. (1996, August). *Racism from a healing perspective for a democratic society.* Paper presented at the Association of Teacher Educators Summer Workshop, Tarpon Springs, FL.

Irvine, J. (1994). *The school failure of African-American students: Perplexing problems and promising practices.* Paper presented at the Education Seminar Series, Indiana University,

Bloomington.

Ladson-Billings, G. (1994). *The dreamkeepers: Successful teachers of African American children.* San Francisco: Jossey-Bass.

Larke, P., Webb-Johnson, G., & Carter, N. (1996). Effective classroom management in culturally diverse classrooms: Strategies for educators. *Teacher Educators Journal, 6*(1), 42-55.

Lasley, T., & Biddle, J. (1996). Teaching students to see beyond themselves. *The Educational Forum, 60*(2), 158-164.

Law, S., & Lane, D. (1987). Multicultural acceptance by teacher education students. *Journal of Instructional Psychology, 14*(1), 3-9.

Lawrence, S. M. (1997). Beyond race awareness. White racial identity and multicultural teaching. *Journal of Teacher Education, 48*(2), 108-117.

Lawrence, S. M., & Bunche, T. (1996). Feeling and dealing: Teaching white students about racial privilege. *Teaching and Teacher Education, 12*(5), 531-543.

Lickona, T. (1988). Educating the moral child. *Principal, 68*(2), 6-10.

McCall, A. L. (1995). Constructing conceptions of multicultural teaching: Preservice teachers' life experiences and teacher education. *Journal of Teacher Education, 46*(5), 340-350.

McDiarmid, G., & Price, J. (1993). Preparing teachers for diversity: A study of student teachers in a multicultural program. In M. O'Hair & S. Odell (Eds.), *Diversity and teaching: ATE yearbook* (pp. 31-59). Fort Worth, TX: Harcourt Brace Jovanovich.

Menz, M. (1996). *Different by design.* New York: Routledge and Kegan Paul.

Mueller, D. (1986). *Measuring social attitudes: A handbook for researchers and practitioners.* New York: Teachers College Press.

National Center for Education Statistics. (1992). *The condition of education.* Washington, DC: U.S. Department of Education, Office of Educational Research and Improvement.

National Education Association. (1996). *Status of the American public school teacher, 1995-96: Highlights.* Washington, DC: Author.

Nel, J. (1993). Preservice teachers' perceptions of the goals of multicultural education: Implications of Cummins' model for teacher education. *Action in Teacher Education, 14*(3), 38-45.

Nieto, S. (1996). *Affirming diversity: The sociopolitical context of multicultural education* (2nd ed.). White Plains, NY: Longman Publishers.

Ogbu, J. (1992). Understanding cultural diversity and learning. *Educational Researcher, 21*, 5-14.

Pajares, M. (1992). Teachers' beliefs and education research: Cleaning up a messy construct. *Review of Educational Research, 62*(3), 307-332.

Pewewardy, C., & Willower, D. (1993). Perceptions of American Indian high school students in public schools. *Equity & Excellence in Education, 26*(1), 52-55.

Rist, R. (1978). *The invisible children: School integration in American society.* Cambridge, MA: Harvard University Press.

Rokeach, M. (1968). *Beliefs, attitudes, and values: A theory of organization and change.* San Francisco: Jossey-Bass.

Scott, R. (1995). Helping teacher education students develop positive attitudes toward ethnic minorities. *Equity & Excellence in Education, 28*(2), 69-73.

Shutiva, C. (1995). Sticks, stones and stereotypes: Native Americans and the curriculum. *Multicultural Education: Issues and Practices, 1*(1), 70-76.

Sleeter, C. (1992). *Keepers of the American dream: A study of staff development and multicultural education.* London: Falmer Press.

Solomon, R. (1995). Beyond prescriptive pedagogy: Teacher inservice education for cultural diversity. *Journal of Teacher Education, 46*(4), 251-258.

Steller, A., & Lambert, W. (1996). Teach the children well. *Executive Educator, 18*(2), 23-28.

Tatum, B. (1992). Talking about race, learning about racism: The application of racial identity development theory in the classroom. *Harvard Education Review, 62*(1), 1-24.

Tierno, M. (1996). Teaching as modeling: The impact of teacher behaviors upon student character formation. *The Educational Forum, 60*(2), 174-180.

Time to bury church's racism. (1996, March 29). *The Atlanta Constitution,* p. A18.

Valli, L. (1995). The dilemma of race: Learning to be color blind and color conscious. *Journal of Teacher Education, 46*(2), 120-129.

Wayson, W. (1988). *Results from a survey of multicultural attitudes and competencies among students completing student teaching from the college of education at Ohio State University, 1985-86.* Columbus, OH: Ohio State University.

Wellman, D. T. (1993). *Portraits of white racism* (2nd ed.). Cambridge: Cambridge University Press.

chapter VI

Issues in Healing Racism in Teaching and Teacher Education: A Case Studies Approach

Fredda D. Carroll, *University of Arkansas at Pine Bluff*
Carol Felder, *Winthrop University*
Phyllis Y. Hammonds, *West Helena, Arkansas*

The racial, ethnic, and linguistic composition of public schools in the United States will be changing rapidly in the near future. By the year 2000, approximately 6 million children with linguistic and cultural differences will be represented in U.S. classrooms (Garcia, 1994; Soto, 1994). In addition, one-half of school-age children will be people of color. What is disturbing, is that most of these children are not likely to have teachers of their same racial or ethnic background.

Eighty-eight percent of teachers in the U.S. are White (Cushner, McClelland, & Safford, 1992). This data reveals the obvious underrepresentation of teachers of color in this nation's schools. Teachers from minority groups are needed to serve as role models for all students, to bring the perspectives of diverse life experiences to the challenging job of teaching, and to create school environments that reflect the values of a diverse society.

Universities are striving to find new methods to help preservice teachers better serve students with diverse backgrounds and experiences (Cabello & Burstein, 1995). Unfortunately, the curriculum often does not acknowledge students' learning styles or needs. Rodriguez and Sjostrom (1995) believe teacher educators must intensify their efforts to provide preservice teachers with the cultural competencies necessary to meet the challenges of the future. Furthermore, if professors are to be role models for their students, they themselves will have to practice what they preach.

The case studies in this chapter represent actual incidents of racism, or perceived racism, within teaching environments. By reading each of the cases and reflecting upon the issues embedded within it, the reader may be better equipped to confront issues that impede the eradication of racism in education, and to develop strategies for eliminating it.

Case Study:
Teacher Education

Background Information. The four African American undergraduate teacher education majors represented in this study are all women in their early 20s and first-generation college students. Their names are Marty, Linda, Lisa, and Kim. They were accustomed to living and going to school in predominantly African American environments. When asked to list the primary language of the family, Marty stated, "English, or more specifically, Black English Vernacular." This is their third year at the university. The university is located in a small town near the lower Mississippi Delta Region, one of the most fertile areas in the United States, rich in culture, tradition, and history. Ironically, it is also one of the most impoverished areas in terms of education, housing, and health. Out of a total of about 400 faculty members, 24 are African American. Half of the African American teaching faculty have received at least one degree from this university. Of the 600 students enrolled in the university's College of Education, 120 are African American. Of that number, approximately 18 have been formally admitted to the teacher education program. There are three African American faculty numbers in the College of Education.

Incident #1. The students felt a prevailing sense of "not being welcome" in their department. They were not concerned so much about grades, but rather, they worried that the deck would be stacked against them so that they would not have a fair chance to succeed. The students point to one event in particular that bordered on intimidation and discrimination. After Kim and other students scored low on a test, the professor lectured the class on dropping the course. During the "lecture," which was delivered every other day for a period of two weeks, the teacher would look directly at Kim. The antipathy appeared so obvious that fellow classmates, Whites in particular, asked Kim if she was failing the course. They had noticed that the teacher always directed this discussion toward her.

After the second essay exam, the professor wrote on Kim's papers, "Not even close!" He did not offer any corrective suggestions, and Kim did not feel comfortable asking him for assistance. It appeared that when African Americans asked questions, the professor did not have enough time to provide substantive answers. When others asked questions, however, the teacher would offer step-by-step responses. Kim dropped the class, stating, "I guess he won after all." Each day, Kim wishes that she had been better prepared to complete the course, but she doesn't feel it would have made a difference—especially "since the instructors don't want me there anyway."

Incident #2. When Marty interviewed for admission into the education program, she was told by one of the professors that there were "provisions for minorities, but that doesn't mean you're going to get in." Marty became angry because she already had been fully admitted to the university, and had maintained a 3.4 grade point average throughout her studies. The minimum GPA requirement for the program is 2.5.

When asked later about how she responded, Marty stated that she had said nothing, which she felt was her only means of controlling her emotions. She could not articulate anything but the rage within. Marty also explained how her instructors disparaged the use of Black English Vernacular (BEV) in the classroom, and that they considered those who used the dialect to be "ignorant and inferior." The students never voiced an opinion or entered into an academic discourse on BEV, but assumed total ownership of the comments voiced in their classes. In addition, the students' attempts to have the instructors answer their questions or explain assignments met with little response; this only helped to further insulate and isolate the students in what they felt to be a hostile environment.

When asked what outcomes they were expecting, what actions they were going to take, if they anticipated any retributions from our conversation, and if they would present these same scenarios to the college grievance committee, the students were hesitant. Eventually, they agreed to go to the grievance committee because they did not want other students to be subjected to the same negative treatment. The conference was scheduled at a "neutral site" on campus so that the students would feel at ease, and confidentiality could be maintained.

Reflective Questions:
• How and/or why did these situations develop?
• What are some underlying factors (personal, institutional) that may have contributed to these cases?
• How might cultural differences between students and professors create misunderstandings?
• How can teachers develop sensitivity for working with diverse students in college classrooms and in public school classrooms?
• What role does the curriculum play in sensitizing students and instructors to cultural differences?

In follow-up talks with the students, three of them found that the amount of negative comments or jokes had decreased. They also believed that the committee had spoken to the instructors, because their presence was acknowledged with courteous nods or smiles. Kim felt that nothing had changed. When asked to share specifically any incidents that she had witnessed, she could only say that she "sensed" it. All of the students have since completed their programs.

Case Study:
Teacher Education

Background Information. These incidents occurred in an education methods class at a state university. The student involved in this incident is an African American female, Angela, who is from a large city. This was the first time she had actively

It appeared that when African Americans asked questions, the professor did not have enough time to provide substantive answers. When others asked questions, however, the teacher would offer step-by-step responses.

interacted with members of other cultures. The professor of the course, Dr. Adams, was a Caucasian male who had taught at the university for 20 years.

Incident. Dr. Adams and his students were in the midst of creating an interdisciplinary unit on holidays as an in-class activity. The final holiday they discussed was Kwanzaa, an African American spiritual holiday. Angela was the only African American student in this class. As the discussion began on Kwanzaa, she was singled out to discuss the purpose of this celebration and the different activities that are conducted during this period. Neither Dr. Adams nor the other students appeared to know anything about Kwanzaa. Dr. Adams said, "Angela, since you are Black, why don't you tell us about Kwanzaa? Tell us what each day means in the celebration and how you and your family celebrate this during the Christmas holidays." Angela was shocked that she was called on suddenly to share this information. She was very uncomfortable and did not know how to respond to the questions. The professor and students were surprised that Angela was unable to provide much information. In fact, Angela and her family do not celebrate Kwanzaa. After this incident, Angela considered dropping the course because she felt that she had been forced to share information only because she was African American. She did not have a close relationship with her professor and did not want to either discuss this incident or continue the class. Dr. Adams did not understand why Angela was so frustrated about the question. He felt that he was including Angela in the class discussion and that the question was an easy one. He also made the mistake of connecting Kwanzaa with Christmas.

Reflective Questions:
• Should Angela have been offended by this question or was she just being defensive?
• Was there anything wrong with Dr. Adams's question?
• What recommendations would you make to Angela about changing her attitude about the incident? What recommendations would you make to Dr. Adams about asking the question?
• How do you think the other students in the class felt about Angela and her inability to answer a question related to her race?
• How could you turn this incident into a positive learning experience in teacher training?

Solutions. The issue that should be discussed, whether at the pre-training level, the inservice level, or the university faculty level, is the "dysconsciousness of racism." Angela does not feel that she should be the spokeswoman for African American traditions. Expecting her to know everything about all the traditions practiced by African Americans put her on the spot unfairly and she felt judged negatively for not being the residential expert on "African American culture." Many students who are in the minority in their classes have been placed in this situation and, as a consequence, they feel more isolated from other members of the class. This type of insensitivity lessens the likelihood that cultural differences will be accepted.

Case Study:
Elementary Education

Background Information. Mrs. Chalk teaches a 4th-grade class in a private school in a small university town. She has been teaching there for approximately six years, and is active in the community. This past year, Mrs. Chalk had a boy named Ernesto in her class, along with 16 other children. Ernesto's father recently opened a law practice in town. Ernesto's mother is Hispanic and his father is of Northern European descent. Ernesto is the only minority group representative in the entire school.

Incident. Ernesto and his family moved to this town at the beginning of the school year. He was very excited about enrolling in his new school and by the possibilities of new friendships and learning experiences. The acknowledged "leader" of this 4th-grade classroom was Ben, a rather aggressive boy. Both Ben and Ernesto are very competitive, but Ernesto was better in some areas, especially sports and math. Shortly after school began, Ben started addressing Ernesto as "Taco." Although Ben was a leader in this classroom, he achieved that position primarily through bullying. Soon Ben had all of the children calling Ernesto "Taco." Ernesto appeared to accept his new name, as he answered to it. He remained friendly and cooperative throughout this time. One day after school, however, he told his mother about the nickname. He wanted to know why they called him "Taco." She was horrified to know that this had occurred and that his teacher had done nothing to stop the children's behavior. She went to school the next day to discuss the incident with Mrs. Chalk. Mrs. Chalk stated that she was not aware of the situation, but would take actions to ensure that Ernesto would be called by his rightful name. Mrs. Chalk held a conference with Ben's mother, who told Mrs. Chalk to do whatever she thought was best. Ben's mother further stated that Ben was constantly in trouble at home and she had no idea what to do in a situation like this

The teacher wanted to give Ben "hands-on experience of being the only different one" in a class. With the permission of Ben's parents, Mrs. Chalk decided to take Ben to a predominantly Black school with her for a full day of "immersion" in a different culture. Ben was permitted to attend classes, lunch, library, and recess in this new setting. Because she had parental support, Mrs. Chalk felt that Ben would see the seriousness of his behavior. Mrs. Chalk admits that this was a very risky action to take, and that she probably could not do this everywhere. She took advantage of her close contact with the parents. The future will determine whether she made a difference in the two children's lives and in the classroom.

Reflective Questions:
- Do you think that the actions taken by the teacher were appropriate? Why? Why not?
- How could Mrs. Chalk have handled this situation differently?
- If you were Ernesto's mother, how would you have reacted?
- Ben's mother apparently accepts the fact that her son is a bully. What are some reasons why she accepts this behavior?
- Why do you suppose Ben's mother agreed to let Mrs. Chalk take Ben to the other school?
- Why do you think Ernesto accepted the nickname without protesting?
- What responsibility does the school have in this particular case?
- What effect to you think this type of "cure" will have on Ben? His classmates? Ernesto?

Case Study:
Early Childhood

Background Information. Mrs. Green's kindergarten class is in a public school in a small university town. Mrs. Green has taught for more than 15 years. She is well thought of in the community and participates in several community activities. One of her students is Maurice Evans, who is the youngest of four children. He attended nursery school and participates in several community youth programs throughout the year. Maurice, who is African American, is a happy, curious young boy. He looks forward to going to school.

Incident. One morning, Maurice's mother drove him to school and walked him to his class, talking to him about all of the fun things he would be learning that day. As Maurice and his mother approached the classroom, Mrs. Green was standing in the doorway, greeting her students. Jenny, a Caucasian female classmate of Maurice's, entered the door before Maurice. Mrs. Green, who is also Caucasian, greeted Jenny by saying, "Good morning, Jenny, you look so pretty this morning. I really like your dress. Go into the class and put your book bag and coat up and then you may go play on the computer." Jenny received a wide, approving smile from Mrs. Green as she walked through the door.

Maurice entered the door next. Mrs. Green turned around to meet the next student and realized that it was Maurice. Her face suddenly changed. There was no smile or show of positive body language that would make Maurice or his mother feel that she was happy to see Maurice. In a firm tone and with an unsmiling face, Mrs. Green greeted Maurice by saying, "Good morning, Maurice. Put your books up and sit at your table."

Maurice was one of three African American males in this class. Maurice's mother watched the smile leave her son's face as he disappointedly walked to the table with the boys. Mrs. Green barely looked at Maurice during this interchange. She turned to greet the next student, but instead found herself facing Maurice's mother, who had observed the incident. Maurice's mother stepped past Mrs. Green and went to her son, hugged and kissed him, telling him to have a good day. This was her way of trying to reverse the negative effects of his experience with Mrs. Green. Mrs. Evans left the classroom, looked at Mrs. Green, and wondered about the best way to address what had just happened to her son. Although Mrs. Evans considered Mrs. Green's behavior during this incident to be racist, she did not want to do anything that would cause her son to suffer more negative treatment.

Reflective Questions:
- How do you think Mrs. Evans felt as she observed what happened to her son?
- What do you think would be the best way for Maurice's mother to address her concerns with Mrs. Green?
- Do you think Maurice's mother is reading more into the incident than was actually meant?
- Is there, or should there be, someone at the school who is objective and easy to communicate with whom Mrs. Evans could talk to so that the teacher, the parent, and the student can find a positive solution? If so, who and why?
- Do you see anything wrong in the way Mrs. Green greets all of her students at the beginning of school?
- Have you had a similar experience happen to you as a child? If so, how did you feel?
- Why do you think Mrs. Green greeted the two students differently? Do you think she was aware of the difference? Explain.
- If you were Mrs. Green's principal or supervisor, what are some concerns you would have about Mrs. Green's behavior?

- In what ways do you think Mrs. Green's behavior will affect Maurice's day at school?
- In what way do you think Maurice will react to Mrs. Green's behavior during class?

Solutions. Education is a joint venture between the community and the schools. All members of the community should have an active role in improving the teaching/learning process. Parents are a vital part of this partnership. Research shows that parent involvement increases the chances that children will reach a higher achievement level. Schools should make every effort to embrace parents and have them feel a part of the education process. When such a partnership does not exist or is not working well, problems occur and children suffer. Mrs. Green's behavior towards Maurice shows a lack of communication or partnership between Mrs. Green and Maurice, and between Mrs. Green and Maurice's parents.

This situation, and similar ones elsewhere, could be addressed in several ways:

- Mrs. Green should address Mrs. Evans's concerns, to clarify any misperceptions of her behavior.
- Maurice's mother could become more actively involved in her son's education, maybe volunteering when possible in her son's classroom, for example, so that she and Mrs. Green can develop a working relationship, and possibly prevent negative incidents like this one from happening again.
- If Mrs. Green had prior problems with Maurice that might have caused her reaction, she should have addressed these issues with the parents as soon as the problem occurred. This way, Maurice's behavior could be remediated, and his parents could be involved in the process.
- Teachers, parents, and university faculty could benefit from working together to develop activities that would train teachers and parents in conflict resolution.
- Students in teacher training should be given extensive experiences in dealing with diversity. Courses in multicultural diversity should be required throughout the student's program. Field experiences with diverse populations should be required.
- Teachers should be given training in communication skills, both verbal and non

> Education is a joint venture between the community and the schools. All members of the community should have an active role in improving the teaching/ learning process.

verbal, as a means to develop and improve their interactions with children and parents.

• Teacher training programs should allow university faculty and teachers to partner within the schools, to improve both teachers' working conditions and their motivation.

Teachers need to feel secure enough to step back and reflect on their actions, and analyze whether their behavior might have contributed to any unpleasant experiences.

Summary

The need for greater sensitivity is a recurring element of all these case studies. In 1993, Recruiting New Teachers, Inc., stressed the need for teachers to be culturally sensitive if students are to thrive and become productive citizens in the 21st century. Rodriguez and Sjostrom (1995) suggest that respect for cultural differences is a prerequisite for good teaching practices in a diverse society. Ladson-Billings (1994) recommends revisiting the teacher education curriculum. In addition, a critical analysis of teacher preparation is imperative for providing models of good practice. To make preservice teachers more sensitive to students' needs, Haberman (1991) suggests the following: "Teach classroom behaviors that support the realization of multiculturalism in the classroom; advise and counsel students as they reflect on their perceptions; and use pedagogical techniques that lead to value shifts" (p. 29).

It is hoped that the case studies presented in this chapter adequately reveal issues of racism that must be confronted by every teacher preparation program. Unless teacher educators accept the reality of racism, new teachers will not learn how to confront this issue in the classroom, nor be able to meet the needs of all students, regardless of their racial, ethnic, or cultural backgrounds.

References

Cabello, B., & Burstein, N. D. (1995). Examining teachers' beliefs about teaching in culturally diverse classrooms. *Journal of Teacher Education, 46*(4), 285-293.

Cushner, K., McClelland, A., & Safford, P. (1992). *Human diversity in education.* New York: McGraw-Hill.

Garcia, E. (1994). *Understanding and meeting the challenge of student cultural diversity.* Boston: Houghton Mifflin.

Haberman, M. (1991). Can cultural awareness be taught in teacher education programs? *Teaching Education, 44*(1), 25-31.

Ladson-Billings, G. (1994). *The dreamkeepers: Successful teachers of African American children.* San Francisco: Jossey-Bass.

Recruiting New Teachers, Inc. (1993). *Careers in teaching handbook.* Belmont, MA: Author.

Rodriguez, Y. E., & Sjostrom, B. R. (1995). Culturally responsive teacher preparation evident in classroom approaches to cultural diversity: A novice and an experienced teacher. *Journal of Teacher Education, 46*(4), 304-311.

Soto, L. D. (1994). Affirming languages and cultures. In C. Bloom, L. Rebhorn, J. Jones, & L. Heaton (Eds.), *Insights on diversity* (p. 35). West Lafayette, IN: Kappa Delta Pi Publications.

chapter VII

Beyond Instructional Racism: The Integrative Curriculum of Brown Barge Middle School

Porter Lee Troutman, Jr., *University of Nevada, Las Vegas*
Richard Powell, Elaine Jarchow, *Texas Tech University*
Linda Fussell, Donna Imatt, *Brown Barge Middle School, Pensacola, FL*

The resurgence of racist culture poses a special challenge to educators for redefining the politics of transformative teaching through a broader notion of what it means critically to engage various sites of learning through which youth learn about knowledge, values, and social identities. (Giroux, 1996, p. 69)

The possibility of a new racism, a more subtle and sophisticated racism, is assumed away as it orders social formations anew. (Goldberg, 1993, p. 8)

TOWARD A SCHOOL CULTURE OF ANTI-RACIST TEACHING

Racism remains a pervasive element in North American society. It continues as a way of understanding and interpreting "otherness," as a way of maintaining the categories of "us" and "them," and as a way of marginalizing and excluding certain societal groups from successfully engaging in specific contexts (including schools). This pervasiveness has led to the institutionalization of racism, in its various forms. One form of institutionalized racism, although at times subtle and, perhaps, even unintentional (Ballenger, 1992; Contreras & Lee, 1990), is school-based instructional racism—the downplaying, if not complete removal, of culture as an organizing principle for classroom curricula and instruction.

As debates about race, ethnicity, multiculturalism, and pluralism escalate (see, for example, Hollinger, 1995; Hughes, 1993; Schlesinger, 1992; West, 1994), society in general, and schools in particular, are increasingly being viewed in terms of race and gender (Goldberg, 1993). Correspondingly, certain societal institutions—including public schools, corporations, government agencies, colleges and universities, and the armed forces—are being encouraged to adopt more actively anti-racist policies.

Despite these efforts, racism continues to shape thinking about how one aligns with others in society. Moreover, instructional racism, as defined in this book, seemingly has a stranglehold on the curricular and instructional practices of many schools. Consequently, content-centered instruction that reflects a White middle-class orientation irrespective of diverse students' racial heritages, family backgrounds, and ethnic communities continues to predominate in many schools (see, for example, Trueba, Jacobs, & Kirton, 1990). Hollins (1996) notes:

Within the United States, the Euro-American middle-class culture is clearly observable as a pervasive force in the school curriculum. The emphasis on European settlement in North America, their world influence, and the marginalizing of other cultural and ethnic groups in the social studies curriculum is a good example of bias in perspective favoring Euro-American culture. (p. 83)

Hollins (1996) and others (e.g., Nieto, 1992; Peshkin, 1992) have expressed concern over the prevailing influence of Euro-American middle-class culture on school curricula, and over the perceived tendency of these curricula to create instructional racism. Indeed, the mounting evidence indicates that students connect more readily with school-based learning contexts, and with the related content, when the classroom curriculum aligns closely with students' backgrounds, as well as with their cultural predispositions for learning (Au, 1980; Ballenger, 1992; Erickson, 1987; Erickson & Mohatt, 1982; Jordan, 1985).

It is clear that educators have a special challenge to redefine teaching, and consequently classroom curriculum, in ways that address instructional racism so that students' backgrounds, and their social identities, become part of classroom instruction. It is also clear that most school systems hinder classroom teachers' potential, and ultimately their willingness, to meet this special challenge (Apple, 1986; Quartz, 1996). Long-standing, mainstream school traditions of content-centeredness, individualization, and ongoing competition can still contribute to instructional racism, and defeat curriculum reform efforts. In addition, practices such as ability tracking, which foster a sense of separateness and otherness among teachers and students (Eckert, 1989; Fine, 1991), are too often entrenched. What emerges is a formidable barrier to curriculum reform in general, and to student-centered and equity-centered curriculum reform in particular (Fullan, 1994; Quartz, 1996).

To overcome such barriers, we must rethink mainstream schooling. As a function of this rethinking, educators at all levels and in all locations will need to alter their habits. Given that the concepts of social equality, justice, and freedom are being reconfigured within a contemporary discourse of pluralism (Giroux, 1996; Greene, 1993), we believe that altering the traditional habits and norms associated with mainstream schooling—the first steps toward overcoming instructional racism—is not optional. One means for moving beyond instructional racism, although certainly not a simple task, is incorporating the concepts of social equality, justice, and freedom into classroom instruction. This means that teachers must first understand the nature of these concepts, and learn how to demonstrate them. Students need to learn how to apply these concepts to their lives in and out of school, not merely recite definitions of them on written tests. This kind of instruction might help both students and teachers become more aware of their place in the larger society, and help them value and affirm human differences. Reaching this outcome would likely foster a way of understanding and interpreting "alike-ness" (rather than "otherness"), a way of maintaining the category of "we" (rather than "us" and "them"), and a way of making all societal groups central to, not marginalized from, classroom-based learning.

Few teachers, we assume, would disagree from an ideological perspective with the changes we are suggesting. When this ideology meets the reality of school classrooms, however, teachers often do not have the leeway to rethink how and what to teach. Most teachers must teach that which is mandated by state agencies; in their schools, the subject matter boundaries are clear and well defined, and Euro-American middle-class values hold center stage. Making incremental changes in such teaching contexts can be difficult, at the very least. And even when incremental changes are put into place, they can be easily lost in the midst of mainstream habits and norms (Quartz, 1996). What is needed, then, is not only a new culture of anti-racist teaching, but also a new culture of anti-racist school reform. What follows is a case report of how one magnet school, Brown Barge Middle School (BBMS), institutionalized a new culture of school reform that provided a context for its teachers to create and implement anti-racist curriculum and instruction.

> **Most teachers must teach that which is mandated by state agencies; in their schools, the subject matter boundaries are clear and well defined, and Euro-American middle-class values hold center stage.**

Curriculum Reform at Brown Barge Middle School

Trying to reform a school curriculum that traditionally has represented a mostly subject-centered orientation can be a formidable task. Several factors of traditional curricula may block reform efforts, including:

- Subject matter that is structured in such a way that it limits how information is presented
- Parents' entrenched preference for traditional, subject-centered curricula
- Some teachers' comfort with using a traditional curriculum, including lesson plans and instructional materials
- The use of textbooks that strongly adhere to traditional content (Cuban, 1992).

Faculty at Brown Barge Middle School (BBMS) decided to bypass the status quo of mainstream schooling in the United States, and instead create, implement, and sustain an integrative curriculum framework. Educators at BBMS completely restructured course content, the relationships between teachers and students, the relationships among students, and the overall outcomes for learning (Powell, Skoog, & Troutman, 1996). BBMS now uses an entirely theme-based, cross-age curriculum based on the curriculum theories of James Beane (1993).

BBMS teachers, like educators elsewhere, must respond to questions of what and how to teach. In many school settings, these questions often are answered first on the basis of traditional subjects (e.g., mathematics, science, history, language arts), and then on the basis of students' needs. At BBMS, however, these questions have been answered first on the basis of the interface between students' personal concerns and society's greater social concerns (Beane, 1993). Consequently, rather than teaching traditional subjects, BBMS educators have implemented a curriculum made up of carefully selected themes, or units of instruction, called "streams" (Barr, 1995). Two streams at BBMS that are central to this chapter are *American Tapestries* and *Conflict and Compromise*.

These streams are 12-week instructional units. During the 1995-96 school year, BBMS offered its students 13 different streams (see Powell, Skoog, & Troutman, 1996, for an overview). Consistent with the suggestions of Beane (1990), the various streams, when studied collectively, provide students with opportunities to build social consciousness and enhance social awareness by studying topics related to contemporary social, environmental, technological, cultural, and ethical issues. Each stream's subject matter is selected on the basis of its relevance to the students' lives. Traditional textbooks are not used.

The *American Tapestries* and *Conflict and Compromise* streams, in addition to other streams such as *Environmentality* and *Global Awareness*, were developed so that BBMS students would have explicit opportunities to explore the idea of democracy as it functions in their daily lives. Streams also help students examine the concept of human dignity (including the notions of freedom, justice, and peace) as it influences their perspectives of other people, and consider the workings and values of diverse cultures as they mingle to create a unique and highly diverse society.

Linda Fussell and Donna Imatt helped develop the integrative curriculum now in place at the school. Linda also helped develop the *American Tapestry* stream, and Donna helped develop the *Conflict and Compromise* stream. Richard Powell, Porter Troutman, and Elaine Jarchow are teacher educators and curriculum theorists who have interacted with the BBMS context for several years. They are convinced that the BBMS curriculum directly addresses, and provides a model for overcoming, instructional racism.

American Tapestry

The overall topic of *American Tapestry* is multicultural studies. All instruction in the stream is based on the premise that the United States always has been a multicultural society. Furthermore, *American Tapestry* instruction is based on the belief that an understanding of diversity and a recognition of the common bonds that unite Americans serve to distinguish and strengthen the nation, as well as promote success, prosperity, and harmony. The intent is to help students broaden their awareness, appreciation, acceptance, and understanding of cultures and ethnic groups. The stream also is designed to help all students develop a fuller understanding of their own cultural and ethnic backgrounds. Banks (1993) claims that this kind of understanding is essential before students can appreciate and accept their own ethnicity, and before they can realize the place of their ethnicity in the greater society.

American Tapestry's learning activities are situated in these comprehensive topical areas: Heritage and Tradition, Struggle for Equality, and Current Issues. These areas emphasize specific content knowledge in the language arts, social studies, mathematics, science, and other knowledge domains. Each knowledge domain is given a rationale and is developed further into specific lessons and related activities. The rationale for the personal development knowledge domain, for example, states that recognizing and valuing diversity promotes understanding and tolerance. *American Tapestry* students following the arts domain study dance, music, visual arts, drama, and crafts from many different cultural groups, thus encouraging further cross-cultural understanding.

To integrate various knowledge domains, *American Tapestry* teachers, like BBMS teachers in other streams, created unique and highly engaging activities called simulations. In one such simulation, students role-play congressional representatives, recent immigrants, and U.S. citizens participating in a congressional hearing to determine whether current immigration laws should be changed. In another simulation, students create an original project that evaluates a significant event in America's struggle for cultural equality and examines how that event affected the way of life in the United States.

Unlike conventional contexts that view diversity issues as something to be tacked onto the prescribed discipline-based curriculum, *American Tapestry* allows teachers to find ways to make subject-centered content relevant to their multicultural content. This is what distinguishes the whole BBMS curriculum context from conventional curriculum contexts. For example, as a prelude to a visit to the George Washington Carver museum, the students try to replicate Carver's science experiments. As another example, history is woven into the *American Tapestry* stream through a study of American immigration. Students study why people came to America, why certain people were more welcome, how Americans used immigrants for personal gain, and so on. Throughout the 12 weeks of instruction, *American Tapestry* students also become familiar with selected languages, including the Cherokee language. Students studying the Civil Rights Movement read essays and other writings by Booker T. Washington and W. E. B. Dubois.

Given the curriculum context of *American Tapestry*, two key questions emerge. How are *American Tapestry* students' cultural heritages made part of the stream's curriculum? Do *American Tapestry* students build a greater multicultural awareness of, and do they acquire a greater acceptance for, other societal groups? To answer these questions, we turn to the transformation and social action approaches to curriculum reform offered by James Banks (1993). These features include infusing multiple perspectives into the curriculum, and making decisions and taking actions on social issues related to the curricular content.

Infusing multiple perspectives. By infusing multiple perspectives into classroom curricula, teachers can help students understand varied points of view concerning the study topic (Banks, 1993). This means that classroom instruction involves "the infusion of various perspectives, frames of references, and content from various groups that will extend students' understandings of the nature, development, and complexity of the U.S. society" (Banks, 1993, p. 203). Multiple perspectives help overcome instructional racism, because students become more aware of multiple identities, and cultural heritage becomes a central part of the curriculum.

One project that students complete in the stream is an evaluation of a significant event in the nation's struggle for cultural equality. Students determine how the event influenced the North American way of life. In another project, one *American Tapestry* teacher helps students explore various minority groups' major contributions in science and mathematics. The project also emphasizes how Native Americans sustained themselves as they were forced to move onto reservations.

American Tapestry teachers design activities that actively engage students in a study of civil rights legislation. Some students may visit a civil rights memorial in Montgomery, Alabama. Another teacher helps students compare and contrast the speeches and writings of Martin Luther King and Malcolm X. Students read additional literature by authors of varied backgrounds and cultural heritages. Students view documentaries of cultural and racial conflicts, and they consider minority groups' contributions to the humanities. Students learn about key civil rights organizations of the 1960s and 1970s. They also study the Japanese internment camps of World War II and explore discrimination against Chinese immigrants during the 19th and 20th centuries. The activities described above, which constitute approximately four weeks of *American Tapestry* instruction, are not added onto other lessons. Rather, these lessons provide the content to integrate and extend knowledge and skills acquired during the remainder of *American Tapestry* instruction.

As students work on their group projects, and as they complete other lessons as a regular part of the stream, they make extensive use of the school's media center, as well as the stream reading list. The list is extensive, contains works of fiction and nonfiction, and represents many perspectives. Students can choose from among the works of Jamake Highwater, Phil Mendez, Yoshiko Uchida, Scott O'Dell, Cesar Chavez, Anne Moody, Martin Luther King, and Peter Krass. In addition to books, multimedia presentations such as the America's Ethnic Heritage Series and other video presentations are available.

Participating in social action. When *American Tapestry* students ask questions pertaining to race, culture, and ethnicity, and when they take action on these questions, they engage in what Banks (1993) calls the social action approach to multicultural curriculum reform. The major goal of social action instruction, which appears to foster the highest levels of multicultural understanding, is educating students in the ways of social criticism, social change, and critical decision-making. *American Tapestry* students are encouraged to ask questions about equity, discrimination, and prejudice as they relate to societal institutions and existing social norms. Students gather data for these questions from the school's media center, from the community, and from various other sources.

To help students gather these data, *American Tapestry* teachers create an open learning environment; the teachers accept being challenged about their own beliefs. As a result, classrooms become forums in which students solve meaningful problems; learning is open, divergent, and negotiable. *American Tapestry* teachers also encourage students to be independent and self-guided learners. As students plan and carry out original projects, teachers are available for consultation and feedback, as needed.

> The major goal of social action instruction, which appears to foster the highest levels of multicultural understanding, is educating students in the ways of social criticism, social change, and critical decision-making.

Conflict and Compromise

Multiple perspectives and social action, two explicit features of the *American Tapestry* stream, are also reflected in the curriculum and instruction of *Conflict and Compromise*, another 12-week unit of instruction at BBMS. Conflict resolution, which is the overarching topic for *Conflict and Compromise*, is studied on local, national, and global levels. Both teachers and students explore various societal groups' cultures, religions, values, and social interactions. Students in *Conflict and Compromise* have various opportunities to examine social identities, including their own, and to learn how these identities can be central to cultural conflict.

The curriculum of *Conflict and Compromise* directly addresses instructional racism through extensive and ongoing activities and simulations related to many societal groups' cultural backgrounds. Indeed, culture is the central organizing principle for the curriculum and instruction.

Premise. The learning experiences in the *Conflict and Compromise* stream are organized around the following premise: When students identify and understand the roots of conflict and the strategies for compromise, they will be better able to develop and implement creative, nonviolent alternatives to interpersonal, intergroup, and international conflicts.

The teachers must create learning experiences that are consistent with the stream's premise. These teachers, however, do not develop this kind of awareness without students' input, as would likely happen in a traditional subject-centered curriculum. BBMS teachers work as co-learners with students. As such, the teachers assume the role of guide and facilitator of student learning, rather than of content expert and authority. Although teachers co-construct learning experiences with students, the teachers also work from a stream document that suggests what simulation activities might be best suited to helping students achieve the overall goal. Sample simulation activities are described below.

Simulations. All students are expected to complete four simulations in the *Conflict and Compromise* stream.

- Plan and implement activities dealing with conflict resolution for Brown Barge 6th-grade students
    - basic concepts of conflict resolution
    - how conflict escalates and de-escalates
    - expressing feelings (especially anger)
    - communication
    - negotiation and mediation
- Create and produce a youth crime and violence task force that provides recommendations for reducing juvenile crime and youth gang activity in the community
- Develop an individual or group project evaluating the causes and effects of World War II
- Enter a research-based historical paper, display board exhibit, dramatic presentation, or media documentary that is focused on the annual National History Day theme in the Brown Barge History Day.

The students work collaboratively on numerous activities and learning experiences. As they prepare for each stream, they acquire content in multiple areas.

Content. Unlike content taught in traditional classrooms, content in the *Conflict and Compromise* stream is selected on the basis of its relevance to the simulations, and relevance to the stream's premise. The content areas (or "knowledge areas," as they are known at BBMS) with which students become familiar during the stream include social studies, media literacy, personal development, language arts, speech and oral presentation, art, dramatic interpretation, physiology, literature, statistics and related mathematics, research, problem-solving, journalism, and science.

When students work toward acquiring the knowledge areas above, they learn basic concepts related to each simulation. For example, as students prepare to complete Simulation I, they identify and illustrate basic concepts of conflict resolution and styles of handling conflict (which pertain to the content areas of sociology and media). As another example, students maintain a conflict journal to record interpersonal conflict and suggest solutions (personal development, language arts). As students work on Simulation II, they debate youth crime issues (social studies, public speaking), analyze statistics, and chart the most common causes of violent crimes (research, mathematics, social studies), and analyze and make charts and graphs based on data about youth violence (mathematics, geography). As students complete Simulation III, they investigate the rise of fascism (comparative government), create and maintain a World War II civilian diary demonstrating the different points of view of Americans, Europeans, and Japanese Americans (history, language arts), and explore the chronology of the Holocaust (social studies, research skills, oral presentation). Simulation IV engages groups of students in original research. After reviewing various resources, students brainstorm areas of interest in historical research. Working together in small groups, students complete historical research on selected topics for which they feel personal ownership. As they work on Simulation IV, teachers in the stream become co-learners with students, since they do not always have the breadth and depth of knowledge about research topics that students eventually develop.

> The potential for overcoming instructional racism is limited unless teachers are willing to view themselves in alternative roles.

Processes for Overcoming Instructional Racism

The two instructional streams at BBMS—*American Tapestry* and *Conflict and Compromise*—demonstrate several key processes that we believe are needed to overcome instructional racism. These elements include (but are not limited to):

- Making students' racial and ethnic backgrounds, in addition to other cultural dimensions of their lives, central to curriculum development and to classroom instruction
- Making students' and teachers' social identities central to curriculum development and to classroom instruction
- Teaching content and skills that typically are not taught in traditional classes
- Teaching about contemporary social and political problems
- Building students' awareness of various aspects of race and ethnicity that cause interpersonal, societal, and international conflict.

The two instructional streams described in this chapter very clearly exemplify the processes above. Teachers' interactions with students, with peers, and with the content must demonstrate their belief in the streams' premises. Teachers also must be willing to be co-learners with students, removing themselves from the traditional role of subject matter expert. The potential for overcoming instructional racism is limited unless teachers are willing to view themselves in alternative roles.

Teachers' Roles in Overcoming Instructional Racism

An essential element for making anti-racist instruction functional at BBMS is teacher commitment, both to the curriculum ideology of the school and to wholesale curriculum reform. This means that teachers at the school must not only be conversant in the theory of integrative curriculum, but also model civil, open-minded social relations.

American Tapestry teachers must be committed to the ideals of multicultural education, and to making students' backgrounds central to classroom instruction. They also must be aware of how their own experiences may influence their ability to implement multicultural education. Moreover, teachers in the *Conflict and Compromise* stream must be committed to the ideals of nonviolent conflict resolution.

Teachers in both streams, as well as teachers in other streams at BBMS, have a special challenge to think first about how to engage students meaningfully in the overarching aim of each stream, and about how they can model the goal and organize classroom content around it. This approach diverges from that used by most traditional subject-centered schools. Teachers in these schools often must conform to local or state mandates on classroom curricula. The integrative curriculum at BBMS allows teachers to implement an alternative curriculum framework, which permits them to address instructional racism, and encourages teachers and students to work together as co-learners on social themes and issues.

Successfully engaging students in meaningful learning about social issues also means engaging them in learning about the "deepest problems of common humanity" (Dewey, 1916, p. 42), which, according to Dewey, should be one of the aims of a democratic education. Students and teachers might not be able to achieve this aim within a highly traditional, subject-centered curriculum that decontextualizes learning from life outside of school. Dewey (1916) argues:

The notion that the essentials of . . . education are the three R's mechanically treated, is based upon the ignorance of the essentials needed for realization of democratic ideals. Unconsciously it assumes that these ideals are unrealizable; it assumes that in the future . . . "making a living" must signify for most men and women doing things which are not significant, freely chosen, or ennobling to those who do them. . . . For preparation of large numbers for a life of this sort . . . are mechanical efficiency in reading, writing, spelling and figuring, together with attainment of a certain amount of . . . "essentials." Such conditions also infect the education called liberal, with illiberality . . . at the expense of not having the enlightenment and discipline which come from concern with the deepest problems of common humanity. *A curriculum which acknowledges the social responsibilities of education must present situations where problems are relevant to the problems of living together, and where observation and information are calculated to develop social insight and interest* [italics added]. (p. 192)

The BBMS curriculum, especially the *American Tapestry* and *Conflict and Compromise* streams, engages students in focusing upon the issues, challenges, problems, and successes of living together in a pluralistic society.

Conclusion

An overall aim of the BBMS curriculum was to create a social community of learners who understand the very roots of societal problems, and who understand their role in both creating and alleviating these problems. To achieve this aim, teachers at the school have implemented a curriculum that truly empowers students as self-guided learners, thus enabling them to become highly independent, collaborative learners. The empowerment process, furthermore, has made students' personal backgrounds and social identities central to classroom instruction, thereby addressing one of the key barriers of instructional racism—the exclusion of culture from school as an organizing principle for curriculum and instruction.

The integrative BBMS curriculum provides an example of systemic school reform that, in addition to providing an alternative model of classroom instruction, has made anti-racist teaching a reality. This reform means that students and teachers at the school engage in learning activities that embrace culture, values, identity development, beliefs, and actions of all learners within the school and community context. By the time they have completed three years of these activities, students are aware of alternative approaches to learning and alternative ways of knowing, thus cultivating critical habits of mind. As reported by Powell and Skoog (1995), when students leave BBMS and re-enter traditional school settings, they have developed a critical consciousness for interacting with others, and for engaging in learning activities.

References

Apple, M. (1986). *Teachers and texts: A political economy of class and gender relations in education.* New York: Routledge.

Au, K. H. (1980). Participation structures in a reading lesson with Hawaiian children: Analysis of a culturally appropriate instructional event. *Anthropology & Education Quarterly, 11*(2), 91-115.

Ballenger, C. (1992). Because you like us: The language of control. *Harvard Educational Review, 62*(2), 199-208.

Banks, J. (1993). Approaches to multicultural curriculum reform. In J. Banks and C. Banks (Eds.), *Multicultural education: Issues and perspectives* (2nd ed.) (pp. 195-214). Boston: Allyn & Bacon.

Barr, C. (1995). Pushing the envelope: What curriculum integration can be. In E. Brazee & J. Capelluti (Eds.), *Dissolving boundaries: Toward an integrative curriculum* (pp. 99-107). Columbus, OH: National Middle School Association.

Beane, J. (1993). *A middle school curriculum: From rhetoric to reality.* Columbus, OH: National Middle School Association.

Contreras, A., & Lee, O. (1990). Differential treatment of students by middle school science teachers: Unintended cultural bias. *Science Education, 74*(4), 433-444.

Cuban, L. (1992). Curriculum stability and change. In P. W. Jackson (Ed.), *Handbook of research on curriculum* (pp. 216-247). New York: Macmillan.

Dewey, J. (1916). *Democracy and education.* New York: The Free Press.

Eckert, P. (1989). *Jocks and burnouts: Social categories and identity in the high school.* New York: Teachers College Press.

Erickson, F. (1987). Transformation and school success: The politics and culture of educational achievement. *Anthropology & Education Quarterly, 18,* 335-356.

Erickson, F., & Mohatt, G. (1982). Cultural organization of participation structures in two classrooms of Indian students. In G. Spindler (Ed.), *Doing the ethnography of schooling: Educational anthropology in action* (pp. 133-174). New York: Holt, Rinehart, and Winston.

Fine, M. (1991). *Framing dropouts: Notes on the politics of an urban public high school.* Albany, NY: State University of New York Press.

Fullan, M. (1994). Coordinating top-down and bottom-up strategies for education reform. In R. Elmore & S. Fuhrman (Eds.), *The governance of curriculum* (pp. 186-202). Alexandria, VA: Association for Supervision and Curriculum Development.

Giroux, H. A. (1996). *Fugitive cultures: Race, violence, & youth.* New York: Routledge.

Goldberg, D. T. (1993). *Racist culture: Philosophy and the politics of meaning.* Cambridge, MA: Blackwell Publishers.

Greene, M. (1993). The passions of pluralism: Multiculturalism and the expanding community. *Educational Researcher, 22*(1), 13-18.

Hollinger, D. A. (1995). *Postethnic America: Beyond multiculturalism.* New York: Basic Books.

Hollins, E. R. (1996). *Culture in school learning: Revealing the deep meaning.* Mahwah, NJ: Lawrence Erlbaum Associates.

Hughes, R. (1993). *Culture of complaint: A passionate look into the ailing heart of America.* New York: Warner Books.

Jordan, C. (1985). Translating culture: From ethnographic information to educational program. *Anthropology & Education Quarterly, 16,* 105-123.

Nieto, S. (1992). *Affirming diversity: The sociopolitical context of multicultural education.* New York: Longman.

Peshkin, A. (1992). The relationship between culture and curriculum: A many fitting thing. In P. W. Jackson (Ed.), *Handbook of research on curriculum* (pp. 248-267). New York: Macmillan.

Powell, R., & Skoog, G. (1995). Students' perspectives on integrative curricula: The case of Brown Barge Middle School. *Research in Middle Level Education Quarterly, 19*(1), 85-114.

Powell, R., Skoog, G., & Troutman, P. (1996). On streams and odysseys: Reflections on reform and research in middle level integrative learning environments. *Research in Middle Level Education Quarterly, 19*(4), 1-30.

Quartz, K. (1996, April). *Becoming better: The struggle to create a new culture of school reform.* Paper presented at the Annual Meeting of the American Educational Research Association, New York.

Schlesinger, A. M. (1992). *The disuniting of America: Reflections of a multicultural society.* New York: W.W. Norton.

Trueba, H. T., Jacobs, L., & Kirton, E. (1990). *Cultural conflict and adaptation: The case of Hmong children in American society.* New York: Falmer Press.

West, C. (1994). *Race matters.* New York: Vintage Books.

Section 3

social perspectives

chapter VIII

Can Technology Deliver on Its Promise of Being the Great Equalizer? Some Reflections on the Participation of Disadvantaged Students in Technology

P. Rudy Mattai, *SUNY - College at Buffalo*
Robert L. Perry, *Eastern Michigan State University*
Walter S. Polka, *Lewiston Porter Central School District*

A current television advertisement boasts that there are "no genders, no infirmities, no races . . . there are only minds . . . on the Internet." While that advertisement may sound wonderful, is it really true? Hawisher and Selfe (1992) refer to such statements as the "rhetoric of technology," which has somewhat engulfed us. This chapter examines the advent of the technological wave, or the "third industrial revolution"; the underlying presumptions made about such an intrusion, particularly in the education field, and more important, the implications for minority students; and some of the suggestions made in the literature for addressing the use of technology so that it will benefit all students. This chapter focuses on the implications of using technology with disadvantaged students; therefore, most of the discussion will be within the context of poor and minority students in the United States. Nevertheless, the implications for students in developing countries are not discounted.

Objective Conditions Underlying the Technological Wave and Disadvantaged Students

W. E. B. DuBois contended that the continuing problem of the 21st century would be that of the "color line." Put rather simply, it was his contention that the issue of race would continue to plague American society. His prophecy has been fulfilled—the issue of race occupies a central role in the analysis of society's socio-economic and political health. Despite the Supreme Court rulings in the watershed case of *Brown v. the Board of Education* (1954), which struck down the theory of "separate and equal," the goal of equality continues to elude us. To further complicate this quest for equality, the technological wave that has ushered in an emphasis on electronic communication poses new questions. Can we ensure equal access to such educational technologies? Is the access to educational technologies predicated on reproduction of dominant ideological notions? In other words, can educational technology deliver on its promise of being the great equalizer? Boyd and Raffel (1992) made some observations about America's urban schools that remain essentially true today. According to them,

The most acute problem in American education today involves the unmet needs of disadvantaged students, who are heavily concentrated in urban school systems. There is a growing concentration of children in central cities at risk of not receiving an education sufficient to help them to enter the mainstream of American society. . . . Our nation's city school systems have a growing concentration of students who are most likely to be below national norms in achievement, have special educational problems, and have language difficulties. (Boyd & Raffel, 1992, pp. 22-23)

This litany of woes refers, to a large extent, to financially underfunded schools and politically disenfranchised students. Consequently, the notion of having sufficient (if any at all) educational technologies present in such environments becomes a real concern. There are two principal issues that come to the fore when considering the use of educational technologies in low socio-economic areas: the financial costs and social adaptation necessary for the acquisition of educational technologies, and the political machinations involved in making the necessary infrastructures available in those areas.

Jeanne Hayes posits a close correlation between race and access to educational technologies. Using Chapter I/Title I Funding and Multicultural Students as surrogates for class and race, Hayes (1995) concludes that,

As with low-income students, students in schools with high percentages of multicultural students have less access to computers. This is not surprising because percentages of Chapter I students and percentages of multicultural students are positively correlated in public schools. However, the disparity between high- and low-multicultural percentages is greater than the disparity between low-wealth and high-wealth schools (Quality Education Data, 1995). In general, the more ethnically diverse a school's population, the less access students have to personal computers. . . . Students' access decreases as the ethnic mix of the school increases. (p. 52)

Access to computers provided by school systems is but one side of the equation. The other side is the ability of minority families to provide access to technology for themselves. Furthermore, computers are but one piece in the realm of educational technology; modems and access to the Internet are essential elements. The cost of all three items is extremely prohibitive, particularly for poor families. A very close correlation exists between race and socioeconomic class; according to the last census, well over one-third of all Black families lives in poverty; nationally, approximately one-tenth of the population lives in poverty. It is of little surprise, therefore, that

In a 1993 survey of 55,000 households, the Census Bureau estimated that 37.5 percent of Whites were using computers, compared with 25 percent of Blacks and 22 percent of Hispanics. The survey also reported that 37.5 percent of White adults had personal computers at home, compared with 13.8 percent of Blacks and 12.9 percent of Hispanics. The numbers indicated that the wealthier the family, the more likely they were to own a computer. (Evans, 1995, p. 45)

This state of affairs has implications beyond the question of who can afford to buy computers. It raises questions of how minority students are socialized to technology. Minority students are unlikely to be exposed to technology at school, and even less likely to have such devices at home. Even when students have the opportunity to use educational technologies, more often than not, unfortunately, their teachers assume that all students will respond uniformly. While it may not be difficult to attract minority students to use computers, it is usually very difficult to sustain their interest in such technologies. The reasons for such alienation from educational technologies might be explained thusly:

> **While it may not be difficult to attract minority students to use computers, it is usually very difficult to sustain their interest in such technologies.**

... if [a school] intends to respect individuality, the underlying assumption is that [students] new/unaccustomed to [educational technologies] must go through an assimilation process. Through this process those who are "different" are welcomed . . . but then [are] expected to blend in—to alter their attitudes and behavior to suit the . . . homogeneous "culture". . . . [However] many [students] are growing increasingly dissatisfied with the assumption that adaption is completely their responsibility or that there is value in only one style. (Liedtke, 1995, p. 12)

What is at stake here is the assimilation of minority students into the dominant culture, something that is constantly pushed on them as the *sine qua non* of both their entrance and successful participation into educational activities. These intensified demands for assimilation present additional problems for minority students and, hence, are likely explanations for minority students' disengagement from educational technologies. The lack of exposure to the culture of educational technologies is exacerbated further by political machinations dealing with the provision of technology. Central to such political machinations is the notion of what Bryant (1995) and others refer to as "redlining in cyberspace." The Clinton Administration, led by Vice President Al Gore, has dedicated resources to the National Information Infrastructure (NII), better known as the "information superhighway." Ostensibly, the NII project has given impetus to the advent of the video dial tone, which would permit telephone companies to offer video programming and computer services. The Center for Media Education is among those groups contending that

. . . those who are not connected to the network will experience a severe information deficit. Almost inevitably, this lack of access will restrict the educational, employment, and political opportunities of the technologically disadvantaged, who, if the pattern of video dial tone proposal holds true, are likely to be the poor and/or minorities. (Quality Education Data, 1995, p. 64)

Although the video dial tone is capable of providing universal services, a huge capital outlay to replace copper coaxial cables with fiber optic cable will be necessary. The possibility for discrimination lies in the decisions about which communities will benefit from such infrastructural changes. So important is this decision that Jeffery Chester, Executive Director of the Center for Media Education, refers to it as the ". . . civil rights issue of the 21st century" (cited in Bryant, 1995, p. 47). The decisions could be heavily influenced by the quest for profit. In other words, the companies that consider possible sites for constructing such infrastructure may very well avoid areas marked by predominantly lower socio-economic or minority populations. Therefore, minorities, ironically, will face great odds against becoming involved with the very emerging technology that is meant to be the "great equalizer."

Some Underlying Ideological Presumptions in the Application of Technology

Several ideological obstacles to making educational technology available to minorities may be insurmountable if not properly addressed. A growing body of literature (Giroux, 1992; Larson & Wilhelm, 1994; LeBlanc, 1990; Mendoza, 1995; Moreau, 1984; Piller, 1992; Pratt, 1987; Selfe & Selfe, 1994; Sheingold, Martin, & Endreweit, 1987; Turkle & Pappert, 1990; Wood, 1992; et al.) eloquently addresses some of these major ideological issues. Selfe and Selfe (1994) present a rather thorough discussion and succinctly sum up some of the issues involved. The following scenario involving English composition teachers may very well be applied to the entire educational enterprise:

For the last decade, English composition teachers have been using computers in classrooms to create electronic forums . . . [that] have the potential for supporting student-centered learning and discursive practices that can be different from, and—some claim—more engaging and democratic than those occurring within traditional classroom settings . . . to create and maintain these communities—to defend their use and value—we have often used what Hawisher and Selfe (1992) have identified as an overly positive "rhetoric of technology" (55) that portrays computer-supported forms as democratic spaces, what Mary Louise Pratt might call "linguistic utopias" (48) within which cues of gender, race, and socio-economic status are minimized; students speak without interruption; and marginalized individuals can acquire more central voices. And if this rhetoric is helpful in that it describes what we want to happen—and sometimes, to some extent does happen—in our classrooms, it is also danger-ous. Through its use, we legitimate the status quo of computer use and, as Hawisher and Selfe note, "delegitimate critique" (53)—thus allowing ourselves to think erroneously that the use of computers and networks provides landscapes that are in Mary Louise Pratt's words, "the same for all players" (38). (Selfe & Selfe, 1994, pp. 483-484)

This chapter will examine the use of the computer for drill vs. creative/critical thinking skills, the use of educational technologies for reproducing dominant ideo-logical perspectives, and the bias of a unilingual approach.

Given the fact that most minority students are also from lower socio-economic families, and that the probability of their having access to educational technologies at home is rather low, it is crucial that they have quality time with technology in formal educational settings. All too often, however, this is not the case, and as Sheingold, Martin, and Endreweit (1987) observe:

. . . in schools with large minority enrollment computers are used primarily to provide basic instruction delivered by drill-and-practice software. . . . In contrast, computer use in majority schools is characterized by its emphasis on the use of computers as a tool to develop higher order literary and cognitive skills as objects of study. (cited in Selfe & Selfe, 1994, p. 485)

Other issues loom as well. An inordinate amount of time must be spent overcoming the technology phobia that many minority students experience. Furthermore, schools do not have enough equipment, nor time to use it. To further compound the problem, that which is taught in a computer lab, for example, cannot be reinforced at home, because these students often lack both computer skills and equipment. Mendoza (1995) posits, "The benefits of computer literacy will only ever be fully realized when it is critical, not just [when] fictional literacy is the goal" (p. 7).

Access to the production of knowledge involved in the technological arena also is limited. What Evans (1995) refers to as "affirmative entrepreneurial opportunities" (p. 45), vis-à-vis producing technology knowledge, is a concern for all minority groups:

[Minorities] must not only become consumers of information but producers as well. They must contribute their share of content relating to [minority communities], so that [minori-ties] are represented aptly as the electronic information infrastructure evolves. Given the difficulty in accessing printed information about [minority groups], there is the very real possibility that cyberspace will inherit those same roadblocks. Today a surfer may be hard pressed to access substantive, organized information on [minorities]: the information may be there, but it will likely be buried under ephemeral or euphemistic descriptions and subheadings. Thus, the literature and cultures of [minority groups] may be lost in cyberspace. (Evans, 1995, p. 46)

The need for culturally responsive engagement in educational technologies is extremely important when one considers that much of that technology originates, and is circumscribed by, what Martin Carnoy (1974) describes as cultural imperialism. Dennis Wood (1992) argues that an undergirding cultural component, derived from the dominant ideological group, gives backing to such technology production. Consequently, the computer interface is not devoid of "coherent sets of stereotyped images" (Selfe & Selfe, 1994, p. 485). Educational technology, by and large, has developed ". . . out of the predominately male, White, middle-class, professional cultures associated with the military-industrial complex—[which have shown] a tendency to value monoculturalism, capitalism, and phallologic thinking" (Selfe & Selfe, 1994, p. 486).

Cameron McCarthy, one of the few prolific scholars to address the issues of racial inequality in education, notes rather aptly that, "Despite comprehensive evidence of glaring disparities in education in the United States, rigorous, durable, and compelling explanations of the reproduction and persistence of racial inequality in schooling [have] been slow in coming" (McCarthy, 1990, p. 35). To a large extent, most analyses of the link between racism and education are born out of either a critique of capitalism (e.g., Bowles & Gintis, 1976; Carnoy, 1974; Jakubowicz, 1985) or studies of the educability of minorities (e.g., Bell, 1975; Hess & Shipman, 1975; Jensen, 1981). All too often, there is a tendency to deflect the discussion away from the strong ideological underpinnings. Little attention is paid to the threat of hegemony and the reproduction of dominant perspectives. Selfe and Selfe (1994) refer to "codification of information" and the "application of related discursive constraints" in reference to the privileged position of standard English as the language of default in software (pp. 486-491). The Eurocentric cultural dominance is guaranteed, primarily because of the presumption that one must not only know the rudiments of the English language, but also have an expertise with and an ideological orientation in the language.

Language is one of the more formidable barriers to equality. English is not the first language of many students in the U.S. public school system. While it may be easy to dismiss the issues of bilingualism/multiculturalism and trivialize the discourse by concluding that standard English, or a close variant of it, is the lingua franca of the nation, many researchers (see specifically the works of Bourdieu & Passeron, 1990; Bernstein, 1970, 1977; et al.) contend that language is more than spoken or written products. Rather, it is a complex cultural network that includes thought processes. Standard English has managed to survive as the language of choice or default. Efforts to incorporate various other languages are only made with the underlying presumption that the user has a fairly high-level command of standard English and can think ideologically within that framework. According to Selfe and Selfe (1994),

This decision to use English as a default language with the custom of identifying non-English language background speakers as a marginalized "Other" and the socio-economic forces that limit access to software in other languages clearly [have] important implications for our educational system, for teachers and for students. In schools, this default position means that students from other races and cultures who hope to use the computer as a tool for empowerment must—at some level—submit to the colonial power of language and adopt English as their primary means of communication, even if this submission is only partial or momentary. (p. 489)

Even educational technologies that involve mathematics and the pure sciences are not without ideology. Without explicitly eliciting notions of capitalism, much of what one is required to execute in accessing such technologies is fraught with a corporate ideological orientation inextricably bound to capitalism. Even more problematic to attempts at providing equal educational opportunity is the notion of knowledge as private property—a cornerstone of capitalism and one that is anathema to viewing knowledge as a commodity to be shared by all. Accordingly,

All of these information products are "owned" by an author who can protect work with a "password" and accord "privileges" to readers according to the relationship and involvement she would like them to have with the text. This commodification of information is also played out at additional levels within computer interfaces. Through interfaces, for example, students now learn to access and depend upon sources like BITNET or Internet, library systems in other states, and information bases around the world for the information they need. These electronic spaces . . . are at the same time becoming more expensive and more rigidly aligned along the related axes of class privilege and capitalism. (Selfe & Selfe, 1994, pp. 487-488)

Standard English has managed to survive as the language of choice or default. Efforts to incorporate various other languages are only made with the underlying presumption that the user has a fairly high-level command of standard English.

Some Suggestions for Addressing the Problem

As dismal as these problems may seem, they are not intractable. At the same time, the authors' attempt to critique the relationship between education and technology should not be interpreted as a disdain for such a relationship, but rather as an attempt to be cognizant of the negative tendencies therein, and to encourage practitioners, in particular, to be mindful of, and seek ways of addressing, such tendencies.

First, we would like to join with a number of scholars and practitioners (e.g., Mendoza, 1995; Selfe & Selfe, 1994; Weizenbaum, 1996) who are vigorously entreating us to go beyond the role of technology users and become critics of technology. To be sure, we need to actively engage in a discussion of the implications of technology for issues of equity and diversity. It is an intense engagement that compels

... both "ownership" and opportunity (Wood, 1992, p. 21). In this sense, ... the "ferocious" (Wood, p. 25) effectiveness of computer interfaces as maps is established as much as by what they do not show about American Culture as by what they do. Primary computer interfaces do not, for example, provide direct evidence of different cultures and races that make up the American social context, nor do they show much evidence of different linguistic groups or groups of different economic status. It is only when we recognize these gestures of omission for what they are, as interested versions of reality, that we can begin to examine the naturalizing functions of computer interfaces and, as educators, break the frame to extend the discursive horizon (Laclau & Mouffe, 1985, p. 19) of the landscape we have created and that, in turn, creates us and the students in our classes. (Selfe & Selfe, 1994, pp. 485-486)

Second, we must come to terms with the vast numbers of disadvantaged students whose most crucial needs are not being addressed. Part of the problem may be attributed to the multitude of challenges these students face. An equally disturbing explanation, however, may be the high attrition rate among urban teachers—particularly those who are best equipped culturally to address such issues. In addition, there is a dire need ". . . to encourage the utilization of information about effective teaching and instructional technology" (Boyd & Raffel, 1992, p. 25). Therefore, school/university/business partnerships are extremely crucial. Urban universities, in particular, should take on the role of providing consulting services to urban schools—not only as advocates in persuading the business community to provide badly needed resources, especially educational technologies, but also as providers of the resources that prepare students and teachers alike to be technology users and critics.

Furthermore, as Boyd and Raffel (1992) rightly contend,

... State universities have a particularly important role to play in taking the research implications the required several steps further. They should continue to bring this information to the pre-service and in-service individuals whom they educate and they should continue to produce school-relevant research. (p. 28)

Finally, suburban school systems that are endowed with a variety of educational technologies and cultural capital could be instrumental in ameliorating unequal conditions in the urban areas. Those suburban schools may benefit tremendously from interacting with populations that are virtually absent from their own environments. The computer may hold the greatest prospects for building understanding among people.

Conclusion

Undoubtedly, educational technologies should not be considered in utopian terms, nor as a panacea for our woes. Neither should they be viewed as some sinister invention. Rather, we must become deliberately conscious of how technology can bring about equity in society. Selfe and Selfe's (1994) admonition to form alliances should be extended, for it is

within these forums—which are often global in their participation—[that we] can encourage discussions that focus on interfaces, language issues, cultural reproduction, learning theories, and critical theories of language use. Through these conversations, [we] can contribute to an increasingly critical awareness of technology issues on the part of individuals involved directly in the design of technology. Such conversations—if they can serve to extend and transform the existing intellectual and political terrain for various groups of people—could have, in Laclau and Mouffe's (1985) words, a "profound subversive power." (pp. 498-499)

Second, we cannot dismiss the ways that technology contributes to institutional racism. We ought to actively point out how privilege, doled out to individuals on the basis of race and class (and usually more on race than class), contributes to the continuing inequity in society.

The pervasiveness and continuing development and application of technology in the world is yet another arena into which those who are interested in bringing about an egalitarian society must become totally immersed. The educational institution is one realm, and an important one, in which this phenomenon takes place. Educators can become more than mere consumers of technology. Multiculturalists may do well to heed Giroux's suggestion:

If an antiracist pedagogy is to have any meaning as a force for creating a democratic society, teachers and students must be given the opportunity to put into effect what they learn outside of the school. In other words, they must be given the opportunity to engage in antiracist struggles in their effort to link schooling with real life, ethical discourse to political action, and classroom relations to a broader notion of cultural politics. (Giroux, 1992, p. 141)

Technology may yet be the great equalizer and provide a functional avenue for addressing the issues of racism within and beyond our society.

References

Bell, R. (1975). Lower class Negro mothers' aspirations for their children. In H. R. Stub (Ed.), *The sociology of education: A sourcebook* (pp. 125-136). Homewood, IL: The Dorsey Press.

Bernstein, B. (1970). *Class, codes and control, Vol. I: Theoretical studies towards a sociology of language.* London: Routledge and Kegan Paul.

Bernstein, B. (1977). *Class, codes and control, Vol. III: Towards a theory of educational transmission.* London: Routledge and Kegan Paul.

Bourdieu, P., & Passeron, J-C. (1990). *Reproduction in education, society, and culture.* Newbury Park, CA: Sage.

Bowles, S., & Gintis, H. (1976). *Schooling in capitalist America.* New York: Basic Books.

Boyd, W. L., & Raffel, J. A. (1992). Urban education today. *Journal of Planning Literature, 5*(1), 22-28.

Brown vs. Board of Education, 347 U.S. 483 (1954).

Bryant, H. (1995). Will there be redlining in cyberspace? *Black Enterprise, 25*(12), 47.

Carnoy, M. (1974). *Education as cultural imperialism.* New York: Davis McKay Company.

Evans, V. T. P. (1995). Black out: Preventing racial discrimination on the net? *Library Journal,* 44-46.

Giroux, H. A. (1992). *Border crossings: Cultural workers and the politics of education.* New York: Routledge.

Hawisher, G. E., & Selfe, C. L. (1992). Voices in college classrooms: The dynamics of electronic discussion? *The Quarterly, 14,* 24-28, 32.

Hayes, G. (1995, October). Equality and technology. *Learning and Lending With Technology,* 51-53.

Hess, R., & Shipman, V. (1975). Early experience and socialization of cognitive modes in children. In H. R. Stub (Ed.), *The sociology of education: A sourcebook* (pp. 95-113). Homewood, IL: The Dorsey Press.

Jakubowicz, A. (1985). State and ethnicity: Multiculturalism as ideology. In F. Rizvi (Ed.), *Multiculturalism as an educational policy.* Geelong, Victoria: Deakin University Press.

Jensen, A. (1981). *Straight talk about mental tests.* New York: Free Press.

Laclau, E., & Mouffe, C. (1985). *Hegemony and socialist strategy: Towards a radical democratic politics.* London: Verso.

Larson, A., & Wilhelm, A. (1994, September). *Latinos and the information superhighway. Policy brief.* Claremont,CA: Thomas Rivera Center.

LeBlanc, P. (1990). Competing ideologies in software design for computer-aided composition. *Computers and Composition, 7,* 8-19.

Liedtke, J. A. (1995, March). Changing the organizational culture: Of technology education to attract minorities and women? *The Technology Teacher,* 9-14.

McCarthy, C. (1990). Rethinking liberal and radical perspectives on racial inequality in schooling: Making the case for nonsynchrony. In N. Hidalgo, C. L. McDowell, & E. V. Siddle (Eds.), *Facing racism in education* (pp. 35-49). Reprint Series No. 21, Harvard Educational Review.

Mendoza, L. (1995, March). *Ethos, ethnicity and the electric classroom: A study in contrasting educational environments.* Paper presented at the Annual Meeting of the Conference on College Composition and Communication, Washington, DC.

Moreau, N.B. (1984). Education, ideology, and class/sex identity. In C. Kramarae (Ed.), *Language and power* (pp. 43-61). Beverly Hills, CA: Sage.

Piller, C. (1992, September) Separate realities: The creation of the technological underclass in America's public schools. *MacWorld,* 218-230.

Pratt, M. L. (1987). Linguistic utopias. In N. Fabb (Ed.), *The linguistics of writing* (pp. 48-66). Manchester University Press.

Quality Education Data. (1995). *Technology in public schools, 1994-95.*

Rizvi, F. (1993). Critical introduction: Researching racism and education. In B. Troyna (Ed.), *Racism and education* (pp. 1-18). Buckingham, England: Open University Press.

Selfe, C. L., & Selfe, Jr., R. T. (1994). The politics of the interface: Power and its exercise in electronic contrast zones. *College Composition and Communication, 45*(4), 480-504.

Sheingold, K., Martin, L. M., & Endreweit, M. W. (1987). Preparing urban teachers for the technological future. In R. D. Pea & K. Sheingold (Eds.), *Mirrors of the mind: Patterns of experience in educational computing* (pp. 67-85). Norwood, NJ: Ablex.

Turkle, S., & Pappert, S. (1990). Epistemological pluralism: Styles and voices within the computer culture. *Signs, 16,* 128-157.

Weizenbaum, J. (1996, October/November). Not without us: A challenge to computer professionals to use their power to bring the present insanity to a halt. *Fellowship,* 8-10.

Wood, D. (1992). *The power of maps.* New York: Guildford.

chapter IX

Who Shall Have the Moral Courage To Heal Racism in America? ATE Keynote Address, February 27, 1996

G. Pritchy Smith
University of North Florida

*The arc of a moral universe is long,
but it bends toward justice.*
Martin Luther King, Jr.

*This final chapter is a transcript of G. Pritchy Smith's keynote address at the 1996
ATE Annual Conference in St. Louis. A fitting ending for this book, it is an invitation
to teacher educators to address bigotry in their lives and in their classrooms. Unlike
the previous chapters in this collection, this chapter is not intended to be a scholarly
treatment of the topic of racism. Its tone is personal and conversational. It speaks to
the heart. With the exception of some introductory remarks that have been edited
from the text and some alterations for the printed form, Smith's address appears as
originally spoken.*

I want to thank Rose Duhon-Sells, President of ATE, and the ATE Planning Committee for 1996, for this opportunity to share some of my thinking about teacher
education and its role in creating a more fair, just, democratic, and anti-racist
society. Before I begin let me say that I consider the opportunity to speak at ATE the
highest honor that I will ever receive in my career as a teacher educator.

By the time I have finished this address, I hope I have convinced most of you that
"the problem of racism" in the United States is the responsibility of us all, most
especially the responsibility of those of us who are White, and absolutely the responsibility of every one of this nation's teacher educators.

I can tell you that I am not going to just "tell us White folks what we ought to do." I
am here to talk to all of us. When I say I am here to speak to all of us, I mean every
person who has ever felt marginalized, every person who has ever felt locked out,

every person who has ever felt like other people considered them "different," low-down," or "no good," simply because somebody else did not like "who we were" or "what we believed." When I say all of us, I also mean those of us who have often felt confused regarding how to do the right thing about racism. But most of all, I mean teacher educators. No matter how different we may be from each other, we are here as well-intentioned people who have dedicated our careers to the preparation of teachers.

I'm going to talk about racism, but not about racism alone. Indeed, it is true that racism cuts deeply into the fabric of this society, but it is the bigger beast of bigotry that wields the sword that continues to prune back this nation—that prevents this nation from flowering into the full democracy it could become. In my mind, bigotry is bigotry—whether it is based on race, ethnicity, or culture, or whether it is based on income level, gender, sexual orientation, or any other characteristic that marks one as "different."

Those of you who have heard me speak before know that I always do two things. The first is that I always tell a story, no matter who the audience is, for I believe it is in the stories and voices of ordinary people that we find the great lessons of life played out. The second thing I do is tell the audience exactly what I'm going to talk about. So, after I have told a story I'm going to ask you to think along with me on two subtopics: 1) how racism and its peculiar characteristics play themselves out in the American education system, from public schools through institutions of higher education, and 2) what teacher education programs must do—what teacher education's responsibilities are—to re-create America as an anti-racist, more fair, just, and democratic society.

The problem of racism in the United States is the responsibility of us all, most especially the responsibility of those of us who are White, and absolutely the responsibility of every one of this nation's teacher educators.

T. J. and the Education of a White Boy

I am not an authority on racism, but I have been affected by it all my life from childhood to the present, and I have thought about racism and education ever since I was an undergraduate student at the University of Texas in 1959. The story I have selected to provide as a context for the "meat" of my address is a personal story. My personal experience, after all, if not the best, is the only lens I have for examining racism. When I first wrote this story a few years ago, I titled it "T. J., a Great Teacher: The Education of a White Boy." It is the story of an experience I had at the University of Texas in the summer of 1959, an experience that would change profoundly for the rest of my life the way I would look at the world around me.

I was enrolled that summer in a Foundations of Education course. In that class was Thomas Jefferson Johnson, who preferred to be called "T. J." for short. For the most part, schools were still segregated in Texas. In fact, in all my 15 years of schooling I had had prior to that class, I had never had an African American classmate. T. J. was my first. In the beginning, perhaps T. J. was only a curiosity to me, but something told me that I wanted to know this young man better. One day on the way to class, T. J. called out to me from where he was sitting under one of those grand spreading oak trees on the University of Texas campus: "Hey, Smith, you want a cup of coffee?" The idea sounded good to me. After all, I was growing up, I was 20 years old, and I was away at college, drinking coffee now like a regular grown-up man, something college students did in those days whether they really liked coffee or not. T. J. pulled from his briefcase a thermos and poured me a cup of coffee. We began to have coffee together under that oak tree almost like a ritual, sometimes before and sometimes after class. At these meetings where we would drink coffee and talk, I learned that T. J. was a French teacher in a segregated Black high school in Abilene, Texas. He was at the University of Texas to complete a degree and get a teaching certificate. I began comparing myself to T. J. I was chagrined that his vocabulary of English words far exceeded mine, and that his pronunciation in French seemed flawless to me, a White boy, who even though I had had 14 credit hours of college-level French, still pronounced "merci beaucoup" as "MUR-SEA BOW-COOO, MAY-MWA-SELLE" with those long flat, dipthonged Texas vowel sounds. I could see that T. J. seemed more sophisticated and more intelligent than me. Sometimes T. J. talked about becoming "a great teacher" as if teaching were a special calling. I had never before heard anyone talk about teaching as T. J. did. And he also said things that frightened me sometimes. He used phrases I had never heard before, like "the movement" and "freedom for the People."

You see, in order to understand the importance of my encounter with T. J., you have to remember what it was like in 1959. Neither T. J. nor I were really supposed to be at the University of Texas—T. J. because he was Black, and I because I was what some of the White fraternity boys called "white trash." After all, I wasn't the son of a banker, a doctor, a lawyer, or some well-to-do business man. I was straight off the farm. I was so politically naive that it hadn't even occurred to me that the reason T. J.

and I were drinking coffee from a thermos bottle was that there were no integrated cafes or lunch counters where the two of us could sit down together in the Austin, Texas, of 1959.

One Friday night about midway through the semester I was strolling by myself down Guadelupe Street, known as "the drag" to college students in those days. As I passed the Longhorn Theatre, a movie house, I noticed a strange phenomenon. The line of people in front of the Longhorn Theatre stretched the entire length of the block, and I noticed the line was really a double line of partners, one Black and one White. Then I heard someone call out, "Pritchy, over here, over here!" I looked around to see T. J. standing in this unusual line of people. I walked over, and he asked, "Why don't you join us, Pritchy?" I asked in return, "What in the world are you doin'?" He retorted, "We're trying to integrate the theatre, fool. This is how it works. You see, we stand in line in tandem, a Black and White, and tie up the line so that people who really want to see the movie give up and go on home instead of standing in line all night to get their tickets. When we get to the ticket window my White partner here asks if he and I can buy a ticket. Of course, the ticket seller always says no and we go back to the end of the line and start over. It's a kind of boycott. The theatre owner is either going to have to integrate the theatre or go broke."

T. J. asked again, "Pritchy, why don't you join us?" I faltered as I tried to speak. I stammered, "I, uh, uh, I don't know. I don't think so. I . . . uh." After all, at 20 years old, I had never in my life taken a public action against anything. I had never even stood up for myself when I had been done a wrong, much less ever stood up against an authority that had done someone else a wrong. I remember clearly how in less than a second, the expression on T. J.'s face changed. His smiling face became stoic and hard. His eyes transformed suddenly from the happy twinkle I had known to a piercing, cold, steely stare. With eyes of ice he looked straight into my eyes and said, "Pritchy, if you are not in this line, you are in the wrong line." Then he looked away from me. I felt my scalp tighten. I felt chills run up my spine. I began to back away, almost stumbling from the impact of his words on me as I continued walking down the street. As I walked, his words kept ringing in my ears. I kept hearing over and over in my head, "Pritchy, if you are not in this line, you are in the wrong line." I thought about those words all weekend, again and again. I tried to understand what was happening inside me. I had no prior social context within which to place this experience. You have to remember that this was prior to Dr. Martin Luther King, Jr. and Montgomery and Selma.

On Monday, I started to class early. I had to see T. J. I went to the oak tree, but T. J. was not there. I went to class. T. J. was not in class. The next class day, T. J. was neither at the oak tree nor in class. A week passed. No T. J. Then the following week, T. J. was seated in the classroom. Acting like nothing had happened the week before, I said, "Hi, T. J. Let's have coffee after class." T. J. didn't look at me. He didn't speak. He looked past me with the same icy eyes I had seen on that Friday night in front of the theatre. After class, without a word he walked past me and out the door. T. J. had cut me out of his world.

Another week passed. Finally, when I could stand the inner turmoil I was feeling no longer, I joined the boycott, an experience that was to affect me forever. Some bad things happened before the protest ended. For example, one night policemen leaped from trucks, swinging their nightsticks. I had never seen policemen swing nightsticks as they plunged into a panicked crowd, hitting men and women in their stomachs and heads. I was terrified by the shrieks and cries from the panicked crowd of protesters, and even more terrified by the blood that was being splattered on me as the police hit people as they were coming closer and closer to me where I was pinned by the crowd against the building. I could see that these uniformed men were not just trying to break up a protest. They wanted to kill us. I was lucky that night. I survived without injury, but it was that night that I realized, for the first time, that police in those days were there to preserve a racist social order, not to protect protesters who were exercising their constitutional right to assemble peacefully.

Not all of the time T. J. and I spent together was as frightful or even as serious, for that matter. Although we worked hard that summer mimeographing and passing out flyers, and always making certain we took our turn at the boycott down at the Longhorn Theatre, we had some fun, too. Some Saturday nights we would go to Floyd's Blue Note Club on the Hill, one of the Black sections of Austin, located near Huston-Tillotson College, Austin's only historically Black college. If we were lucky, we might catch someone famous like Jimmy Reed wailing his own kind of blues, live, at Floyd's. After Floyd's closed at about 2:00 a.m., we would cap off the night at Earl's Chicken Shack, an after-hours club where two hungry under-aged young men could eat and get one last drink before the sun came up.

On other occasions, T. J. would be in one of his mischievous moods. During these times, he would pull some prank on me, stamp both feet like he was going to laugh himself to death, and then say, "Smith, you are one dumb White boy." I didn't mind, though. Somehow it didn't seem like an insult.

At the end of that hot summer, in August, T. J. and I parted ways. T. J. had to return to Abilene to start a new school year, even though, as T. J. said, "Most of the kids at the Negro School will be picking cotton until the end of September." We met one last time under the oak tree. The Longhorn Theatre was still segregated. We felt surrounded by the kind of sadness a person experiences when he tries as hard as he can but doesn't win, the sadness of an unachieved triumph. It was the feeling Langston Hughes must have been trying to capture when he wrote about "a dream deferred." As hard as we had tried, we felt like we had failed. We didn't know at that moment that it would be nearly another year before the owner of the Longhorn Theatre would stand before the crowd of protesters to announce that henceforth the doors of the theatre would be open to all. It would be a great moment of triumph, with the crowd cheering and tossing their caps and signs into the air—a moment of joy that T. J. would not be there to experience.

We had met at the oak tree to have one last cup of coffee and say good-bye, but we didn't know how. When it became time for T. J. to leave, there was an awkward, uneasy moment, as if both of us were groping for some words that would sound right—like so often happens when men "just don't know how to act." Then, T. J.

broke the silence and said, "Smith, you're O.K. for a White boy. You're gonna be alright."

I stood there a good long while watching T. J. grow smaller as he walked down the street toward the bus station. I remember feeling like something in the world had changed that summer—like I wasn't ever going to be the same again, like maybe I knew for the first time that people have a choice. They can stand in the wrong line. Or they can stand in the right line.

On that last day I would see T. J., there was no way we could have known that T. J., just five years later, would be killed in the Vietnam War. It was just a few years ago, in fact, that I found myself standing before the Vietnam Memorial in Washington, D.C., weeping almost uncontrollably as I touched my fingers to the letters of his name carved in the stone. The only words I could whisper aloud were "T. J., you did become a great teacher."

I learned many things from T. J. and our experience with the boycott, far too many things, in fact, than I can tell about. However, the most important thing I learned was about myself. I found out that it would take far more than just learning how to drink coffee to become a man. I learned that "I could not stand up as a man until I stood up, first, for someone else," that "I would not become a man until I stood against injustice." It was this single lesson that would enable me later on in life to understand the full meaning of Martin Niemoller's famous words when I would read them for the first time. I am referring to Niemoller's (1968) passage about his inaction in Nazi Germany when he said:

First they came for the Jews and I did not speak out because I was not a Jew. Then they came for the communists and I did not speak out because I was not a communist. Then they came for the trade unionists and I did not speak out because I was not a trade unionist. Then they came for me, and there was nobody left to speak out for me. (p. 31636)

I found out that it would take far more than just learning how to drink coffee to become a man. I learned that "I could not stand up as a man until I stood up, first, for someone else," that "I would not become a man until I stood against injustice."

The experience taught me also to question this society. It also enabled me to begin to understand what James Baldwin (1963) was saying in his famous speech, "A Talk to Teachers," when he said:

Now if I were a teacher . . . dealing with Negro children . . . I would try to teach them . . . that those streets, those houses, those dangers, those agonies by which they are surrounded are criminal. . . . I would teach [the Negro child] that he doesn't have to be bound by the expediencies of any given [government] Administration, any given policy, any given time—that he has the right and the necessity to examine everything. (p. 60)

The experience helped me understand what Lerone Bennett, the African American historian, meant when he wrote that "an educator in a system of oppression is either a revolutionary or an oppressor" (as cited in Hale, 1978, p. 7). It was my experience at the University of Texas that enabled me not to respond to James Baldwin and Lerone Bennett by calling them "radical" or "militant," as did so many of my peers, but to respond, instead, by beginning to question the injustices in this society.

Ultimately, my experience with T. J., along with other experiences, would lead to my belief that teacher education must be multicultural and social reconstructionist. So, therein lies the thesis of my address—in the story I have just told lies the genesis of my thinking about what the responsibilities are of teacher education programs to heal the racism that makes a mockery of this democratic society. Many times since I first met T. J., over 37 years ago, I have asked myself why I learned more lessons about racism outside the classroom than in the classroom at the University of Texas. I've asked myself, "Why has racism been a taboo topic in a teacher's education?" Today, there seems to be a considerable amount of disagreement in our profession as to what a teacher should know and believe about racism.

So, let me turn from the story of T. J. to the substance of my address, which is an attempt to answer the question, "Who shall have the moral courage to heal racism and bigotry in America?"

Who Shall Have the Moral Courage To Heal Racism and Bigotry in America?

Before we can begin to answer the question—Who shall have the moral courage to heal racism and bigotry in America?—we must examine the nature of racism, not only with regard to how racism has played itself out in the history of the United States, but also some of the peculiar characteristics of racism.

The first peculiar characteristic of racism is its historical tenacity. Racism is a very old problem. It has been with us in the Americas since the first Europeans set foot here. Despite the presence of some European Americans who always fought against racism, it has found expression in the official U.S. government policy of genocide in the treatment of First Americans, the enslavement of people of African descent, the Chinese Exclusion Act, the internment of Japanese Americans and seizure of their property during World War II, and the almost continuous resistance to civil rights for people of color in the United States. Although it is an old problem that has been ignored, particularly in our history books, it hasn't gone away. Loewen's (1995) study of the 12 most frequently used high school American history books found that only one linked slavery to White racism. I suspect that when W. E. B. Dubois (1968) said 100 years ago that "the problem of the 20th century is the problem of the color line" (p. 221), he had no idea that the color line would also be the great problem of the 21st century. Racism seems not to be the type of problem that goes away if we ignore it.

In addition to being a very "old problem," a second peculiar characteristic of racism is that it is a problem that so many people deny even exists, no matter how much experiential or empirical evidence proves its existence.

On the one hand, people like Morris Dees (1996) of the Southern Poverty Law Center remind us almost daily that racism and bigotry run rampant in American society. Consider these recent events in public schools:

- In suburban Greenwich, Connecticut, five White high school students encode the words "Kill All Niggers" into the school's yearbook captions.
- Some students at Manhattan's Norman Thomas High School send a Jewish teacher a note that includes a swastika and the words "Kill All the Jews."
- The principal of Randolph County High School in Alabama in 1994 threatens to cancel a high school prom because interracial couples might attend; [he also] refers to a mixed race student as a "mistake" her . . . parents shouldn't have made.
- In Lake County, Florida, the school board, controlled by Christian Fundamentalists, votes that teachers must teach that "America is a superior culture."

Consider, also, that hate crimes and harassment based on race have steadily been reported since the mid-1980s with increasing, not diminishing, frequency on university and college campuses, some of which are considered the most prestigious of our institutions (Lennon, 1991).

Consider this list of events in larger society:

- The FBI reported over "7,000 victims of hate crimes in 1994 alone" (Dees, 1996, p. 4).
- Studies continue to show that prestigious banks and loan institutions continue to disapprove mortgage loan applications on the basis of race.
- Television sting operations continue to expose employment agencies, realtors, and property and rental companies that discriminate on the basis of race.
- In February 1996, a White law enforcement officer in the state of Maryland refuses to give mouth-to-mouth resuscitation to an African American woman; she [later] dies.
- National leaders show no shame in showing their bigotry in public. As Dees notes, "Republican Senator Alphonse D'Amato mocks 'little Judge Ito' " (Dees, 1996, p. 4). Republican House majority whip Dick Armey "refers to his Congressional colleague Barney Frank as 'Barney Fag' "; and "Republican Presidential contender Bob Dornan calls some of his political adversaries 'lesbian spear chuckers' " (Dees, 1996, p. 4).

With this kind of misguided moral leadership among political leaders, who shall have the moral courage to heal racism in America?

On the other hand, despite the evidence to the contrary, a majority of White Americans deny the existence of racism and bigotry and deny the resulting effect of discrimination. For example, The National Conference (1994) survey on intergroup relations, titled *Taking America's Pulse*, found that a majority of White Americans believe that citizens of color in the United States simply are not discriminated against. The same poll, however, found that African Americans, Latino Americans, and Asian Americans believe just the opposite—that bigotry and discrimination continue to be the reality.

In addition to being a very old problem, and a problem that people deny exists, a third peculiar characteristic of racism is that it is a problem that no one seems to own. Although the same National Conference poll found that prejudice against other racial groups exists in all ethnic and racial groups, most of the research tells us that it is only a minority of Americans who will admit to being prejudiced. White Americans are less likely than persons of color to own up to and admit their prejudices. For example, another poll found that only 21 percent of White Americans would go on record as considering themselves biased against people of other races, but that twice as many African Americans (41 percent) would claim their prejudices (Edwards, 1995).

Well, there you have it—the enigma and irrationality of racism. In short, what I have just said is that here we have a very old, non-existing problem that no one owns. So, who shall have the moral courage to heal this old, non-existing problem that no one owns? If the answer to this question is teacher educators, let us examine our students in teacher education for a moment.

Our Students

By now, we teacher educators can almost quote from memory Nancy Zimpher's (1989) well-known and often referenced profile of the typical preservice teacher. That is, that the typical preservice teacher in the United States is a monolingual White female from a low-middle or middle class suburban or rural home who wants to teach children who are just like herself. Other demographic profiles tell us that 90 percent of preservice teachers in the United States are White and less than 10 percent are students of color (American Association of Colleges for Teacher Education, 1987). Research tells us that many preservice teachers simply do not have the prerequisite attitudes or lifestyle patterns regarding diversity that would enable them to teach children who are different from themselves (Ahlquist, 1991; Beyer, 1991; Ladson-Billings, 1991). In fact, most preservice teachers say they don't want to teach minority children, "except as a last resort" (Contreras, 1988). In truth, most students were socialized by their families to live monoracial and monocultural lifestyles as the preferred norm. Other studies tell us that a majority of preservice teachers in the United States believe that the home background of minority public school students is so bad that it just can't be overcome by education. Personally, I am far less worried about the home backgrounds of minority students in schools than I am about the "backgrounds" of cultural and racial illiteracy of teacher education students. Finally, another body of research literature tells us that the attitudes and lifestyle patterns of preservice teachers are extremely resistant to change (Grant & Secada, 1990).

Some of us are shocked—astounded, sometimes—by the depth of bigotry among so many preservice teachers presently in training. My own assessment of today's preservice teachers in undergraduate training is that among them is the largest, most outspoken group of racists I have encountered since the beginning of my teaching career at the university level in 1967. Not all students are racists, of course, but too many are. From my own university classroom experiences, my estimate is that about one-third of U.S. teacher education students are hard-core, intractable racists. Another third of them I would classify as moderate racists, young people who are relatively unaware of their racism, who, in fact, are blind to their own racism, and haven't even given much thought to their racial attitudes. Another 20 percent I would classify as non-racists, young people whom we might describe as good kids who want to do the right thing, but are rather passive and quiet about their thoughts on race. Another 10 to 12 percent, perhaps 3 or 4 out of every class of 30, arrive in my classes as anti-racists, young people who have the prerequisite belief system to become

So, who shall have the moral courage to heal this old, non-existing problem that no one owns?

social reconstructionists—young people who want to reconstruct a fairer, more just, anti-racist democracy.

This profile of the preservice teacher begs us to ask the question, "Who shall have the moral courage to heal racism in America?"

Ourselves,
Teacher Educators

Let's turn from students for a moment and look at ourselves—the teacher educators. If we are honest with ourselves, we are very much like our students, the preservice teachers. Ninety-five percent of us are White European Americans, and as Haberman (1992) has noted, less than 5 percent of us have taught in an "urban" school, and only 10 percent of the universities where we work are located in the great urban centers of racial and cultural diversity. Most of us are monolingual and live monocultural lifestyles. Our closest friends are likely to be of the same race, we are likely to attend same-race churches, live in same-race neighborhoods, and send our children to predominantly White, middle class suburban schools with limited racial integration. Yet, like our teacher education students, some of us depart from this profile norm.

Who, then, shall have the moral courage to heal racism in America? If the answer to this question is teacher educators, what, then, must we do?

What Must
Teacher Educators Do?

Many of us agonize over this "race thing." We agonize over the moral dilemma we face each year when we graduate teachers whose racism and other forms of bigotry are so strong and deep that they cannot help but do damage to the children they will teach. What must teacher education programs and teacher educators do to prepare anti-racist teachers for diverse classrooms? I can tell you it will take far more than just "culturally diverse field experiences," such as those prescribed by the NCATE standards (1995).

First, we must take ownership of this problem, this disease we call racism and its related viruses that constitute the many mutations of bigotry. And we must set goals and missions for our teacher education programs that clearly state that we are not willing to accept "the minimum standard" of teachers who are just tolerant and without bias, but that we intend to graduate teachers who are anti-racists, who are social activists against bigotry—teachers who will create a new world order where racism and bigotry are unacceptable. My point here is that our mission statements should express the moral imperative that we are not preparing teachers to teach in the world as it is, but we are preparing teachers to change that world.

The second thing we must do is infuse what I call "the knowledge bases for diversity" into the center and forefront of the teacher education curriculum. I cannot describe all 13 of these knowledge bases here in detail. Let me simply refer you to the description of these knowledge bases in my book, *Common Sense About Uncommon Knowledge* (Smith, 1998), published by the American Association of Colleges of Teacher Education. I must, however, take enough time to describe two of these 13 knowledge bases.

The first knowledge base I speak of is the one I have called in my writings "Knowledge Base 8: The Foundations of Racism." No teacher should graduate from a teacher preparation program without having thoroughly studied the foundations of racism. In this knowledge base, preservice teachers must:

- Study the true history of prejudice, discrimination, and racism in the United States
- Study the theory and research on how racism is integrated into one's identity and personality structure
- Study the effects of racism on members of the dominant White culture and on members of minority cultures
- Study the theory and research on "changing bigoted attitudes"
- Examine a variety of anti-bias and anti-racist curricula that have been developed for use in the K-12 school curriculum.

In addition to the knowledge base on racism and other forms of bigotry, we must infuse into our teacher education programs the knowledge base on the educational policies and practices that are harmful to minority and low-income students—what I have called "Knowledge Base 9" in my scholarship. This knowledge base enables preservice teachers to understand institutionalized racism and other forms of institutionalized bigotry in the educational system. In this knowledge base, preservice teachers must study the research on the harmful and inequitable effects of using standardized tests to allocate educational opportunity, tests that favor the White middle class and disproportionately disfavor minorities and low-income students. They must study the use of ability grouping and curriculum tracking to racially segregate [students] under the same school roof. They must study the negative effects of racially segregated schools. They must study the use of inequitable funding formulas that cheat minority and low-income students, and study the use of school choice, privatization, and vouchers to create even greater inequities and racial segregation in the educational system. In short, this is the knowledge base that exposes attempts of those who have power and privilege to create a meritocratic, rather than a democratic, educational system.

As we teacher educators present these two knowledge bases, we must own up to our own absence of courage to root out the racism and bigotry that are institutionalized in our own admission and certification policies, which use standardized instruments that have no predictive validity, but have, as my own research has found, eliminated over 100,000 minority candidates from the teaching profession (Smith, 1988).

If we teacher educators do not do these things, then who will have the moral courage to heal racism in this society?

Finally, let me turn to what we teacher educators must do at a personal level, as individuals. Over the long term, what we teach may not be nearly as powerful as what we model. It is likely that long after our teacher education students have forgotten the specific facts, the formal theories, and the

> My point here is that our mission statements should express the moral imperative that we are not preparing teachers to teach in the world as it is, but we are preparing teachers to change that world.

bodies of research on racism as a knowledge base, what they will remember most of all is how we professors of education lived our personal lives. So it is important that we model a multicultural and multiracial lifestyle. It is important for our students to see us having interracial friendships. It is important for our students to see that not only do we believe that a racially integrated education is superior to a segregated education, but that we actually send our children to integrated schools. And, most important of all, our teacher education students must see us not merely as non-racists, but they must see that we are anti-racists, actively engaged in our communities fighting racism and other forms of bigotry. In the final analysis, we must look into ourselves—as Gandhi put it, "We must be the change we wish to see in the world."

Conclusion

We teacher educators have a vision of what America can become. We believe that education can be a powerful force to make this a more democratic society. And yet, that vision is in danger today. I don't have to tell the committed that these are turbulent political times and, as Carl Grant (1992) has said, times in which "we are in a war for the minds of our children."

America stands at a crossroads today. We shall either become a great multicultural society—the first truly multicultural and multiracial democracy on the planet—or we shall revert to our most sinister persona that describes the worst part of our historical past—a compassionless society in which only the elite have power and privilege and in which we judge people not by the content of their character, but by their race, their culture, their gender, their exceptionality, or their sexual orientation. We can be a better nation than that.

It will not be easy to do what we must do. But if we change the knowledge bases our preservice teachers study, and if we, ourselves, model an anti-racist lifestyle, we will give the next generations of preservice teachers the moral courage they need to do likewise. No one has described what we must do any better than Robert F. Kennedy (1966) when he said,

Each time a person stands for an ideal, or acts to improve the lot of others, or strikes out against injustice, he or she sends forth a tiny ripple of hope. And crossing each other from a million different centers of energy and daring, those ripples build a current that can sweep down the mightiest walls of oppression and resistance. Few are willing to embrace the disapproval of their fellows, the censure of their colleagues, the wrath of their society. Moral courage is a rarer commodity than bravery in battle or great intelligence. Yet it is the one essential vital quality for those who seek to change a world that yields most painfully to change.

So, who shall have the moral courage to heal racism in America?

The answer is "us"—we teacher educators. It is the only answer we can afford to give. It is from us that the next generation of teachers and their students must learn the simple lesson that T. J., that great teacher, taught so well—"If you are not in this line, you are in the wrong line."

References

Ahlquist, R. (1991). Position and imposition: Power in a multicultural foundations class. *Journal of Negro Education, 60*(2), 158-169.

American Association of Colleges for Teacher Education. (1987). *Teaching teachers: Facts and figures.* Washington, DC: Author.

Baldwin, J. (1963, December 21). A talk to teachers. *Saturday Review,* pp. 42-44, 60.

Beyer, L. E. (1991). Teacher education, reflective inquiry, and moral action. In B. R. Tabachnick and K. M. Zeichner (Eds.), *Inquiry-oriented practice in teacher education* (pp. 113-129). New York: Falmer Press.

Contreras, A. (1988). Multicultural attitudes and knowledge of education students at a midwestern university. In C.A. Heid (Ed.), *Multicultural education: Knowledge and perceptions* (pp. 63-78). Bloomington, IN: Indiana University, Center for Urban and Multicultural Education.

Dees, M. (1996). Break the chain. *Teaching Tolerance, 5*(1), 4.

Dubois, W. E. B. (1968). The souls of Black folks. In *Three Negro classics* (p. 221). New York: Avon. (Original work published 1905)

Edwards, A. (1995, November 10). Race in America. *Family Circle,* pp. 83-84, 86-87.

Grant, C. (1992). Unpublished speech. ATE Summer Workshop, University of Wisconsin, Parkside.

Grant, C.A., & Secada, W. G. (1990). Preparing teachers for cultural diversity. In W. R. Houston, M. Haberman, & J. Sikula (Eds.), *Handbook of research on teacher education* (pp. 403-422). New York: Macmillan.

Haberman, M. (1992). Unpublished speech. ATE Summer Workshop, University of Wisconsin, Parkside.

Hale, J. (1978). Cultural influences on learning styles of Afro-American children. In L. Morris (Ed.), *Extracting learning styles from social/cultural diversity* (pp. 7-27). Norman, OK: Southwest Teacher Corps Network (Grant No. G007-700-119, Teacher Corps, U.S. Office of Education, Department of Health, Education, and Welfare).

Kennedy, R. F. (1966, June 6). *Day of Affirmation address.* Capetown, South Africa: University of Capetown.

Ladson-Billings, G. (1991, April). *When difference means disaster: Reflections on a teacher education strategy for countering resistance to diversity.* Paper presented at the annual meeting of the American Educational Research Association, Chicago, IL.

Lennon, T. (Producer) (1988). *Racism 101* (video recording). (Available from PBS Video, Alexandria, VA)

Loewen, J. W. (1995). *Lies my teacher told me: Everything your American history textbook got wrong.* New York: New Press.

Niemoller, M. (1968). Testimony before Congress. *Congressional Record,* October 14, 1968, p. 31636.

Smith, G. P. (1998). *Common sense about uncommon knowledge: The knowledge bases for diversity.* Washington, DC: American Association of Colleges for Teacher Education.

Smith, G. P. (1988, Spring). Tomorow's white teachers: A response to the Holmes Group. *Journal of Negro Education, 58*(2), 178-194.

The National Conference. (1994). *Taking America's pulse: A summary report of The National Conference survey on intergroup relations.* New York: Author.

Zimpher, N. (1989). The RATE Project: A profile of teacher education students. *Journal of Teacher Education, 40*(6), 27-30.

about the authors and editors

Mary G. Anderson

Mary G. Anderson is an Associate Professor at the City University of New York, New York City. She teaches special education courses. Her primary research focus is the use of theater communication arts to facilitate and enhance critical thinking and proactive decision-making among students identified as having serious emotional disturbances, as well as among their non-labeled peers.

H. Prentice Baptiste, Jr.

H. Prentice Baptiste, Jr., is Dean and Professor, College of Education, New Mexico State University, Las Cruces. Prior to his present position, he was Professor in Foundations and Adult Education, Associate Director of the Center for Science Education, and Program Planner for the Midwest Desegregation Assistance Center, College of Education at Kansas State University. His research interest includes the conceptualization of multicultural education, the process of multiculturalizing educational entities, and culturally diversifying science and math instruction. Baptiste has authored or edited six books, as well as numerous articles, papers, and chapters on multicultural education and science education. He works extensively with urban and rural schools and school districts in designing and implementing comprehensive multicultural plans. He has presented papers and conducted workshops in Egypt, Germany, Jamaica, Morocco, and the Netherlands.

James B. Boyer

James B. Boyer is Professor of Curriculum & American Ethnic Studies at Kansas State University, Manhattan. In additional, he coordinates the Urban Master's Program for Educators in Kansas City. His research interests include issues of diversity in curriculum and policy studies, along with his continuing work on instruction with culturally different learners. His recent publications include *Transforming the Curriculum for Multicultural Understandings: A Practitioner's Handbook*, co-authored with H. Prentice Baptiste, Jr. (published by Caddo Gap Press, San Francisco). He also has served as major adviser for more than 40 doctoral candidates during his tenure at Kansas State University, while serving as a consultant to numerous school districts and other agencies.

Gwendolyn Duhon Boudreaux

Gwendolyn Duhon Boudreaux is an Assistant Professor in the Department of Teacher Education at McNeese State University, Lake Charles, Louisiana. She teaches graduate and undergraduate courses in education. Her professional interests include post-baccalaureate certification, peace education, and professional development. She has authored or co-authored several articles and book chapters on various topics, such as domestic violence, school violence, racism, peace education, professional ethics, alternative certification, and student empowerment.

Fredda D. Carroll

Fredda Carroll is Assistant to the Dean for Cultural Diversity Initiatives and Assistant Professor of Elementary Education at Arkansas State University, Jonesboro. She holds degrees from Arkansas State University and George Peabody College for Teachers of Vanderbilt University. Carroll teaches graduate and undergraduate courses in education, and is responsible for the recruitment of undergraduate and graduate students in the College of Education. In addition, she has developed undergraduate and graduate courses in multicultural education. Finally, Carroll has secured grant funds for the Minority Teacher Scholars Program, a mentoring program for students of color in the College of Education, and, with others, has secured grant funds to establish the Arkansas State University Summer Academy for Future Teachers, a residence program for high school juniors and seniors who are interested in a teaching career. Its major goal is to recruit students of color into the College of Education at Arkansas State University.

Norvella P. Carter

Norvella P. Carter is Associate Professor in the Department of Educational Curriculum and Instruction at Texas A&M University, Colege Station. She teaches graduate and undergraduate courses in teacher education, urban studies, multicultural education, and supervision. While at Illinois State University, she served as Director of the Multicultural Mentorship Project, a program that gives college students an opportunity to mentor children in the city of Chicago. She is a consultant for Chicago Public Schools and has conducted research in various urban settings in the United States and Europe. At ISU she was a coordinator for school/university partnerships with urban schools, and she works with the team that will design several professional development schools in Chicago. Carter has authored a number of publications that deal with issues of diversity, and she is editor of a book on African American women. Her professional interests include urban education, professional development schools, and international studies.

Alice Duhon-Ross

Alice Duhon-Ross is an Assistant Professor in the Department of Curriculum and Instruction in the school counseling program at Albany State University in Albany, Georgia. She is currently serving as the State and National Unit's Accreditation Coordinator. Duhon-Ross also is on the Board of Examiners for the National Council for Accreditation of Teacher Education (NCATE). Her professional interests include social studies and multicultural education, school counseling, reading for infants, and school violence.

Rose M. Duhon-Sells

Rose M. Duhon-Sells serves as Chairperson of the NAACP Education Committee for the Lake Charles, Louisiana, chapter. She is Founder and first President of the National Association for Multicultural Education. In 1995, she was the first Louisianan and the first African American to be elected National President of the Association of Teacher Educators in the organization's 76-year history. She has over 23 years of experience as a professional educator, including as a Head Start teacher, elementary school teacher, mental health counselor, superintendent, professor, and university dean. Duhon-Sells has published on the following topics: youth violence, multicultural education, family life education, and parental skills for parents of color. Her most recent publication is titled *Peace Education Focused on Self Science*. Currently, she is a professor in the College of Education at McNeese State University, Lake Charles, Louisiana.

Carol Felder

Carol Felder is an Assistant Professor in the College of Education at Winthrop University, Rock Hill, South Carolina. She has coordinated recruitment and retention initiatives for minority students in teacher education programs, and has coordinated grants to encourage minority high school students in urban areas to become teacher education majors. Her professional interests include the recruitment and retention of minorities in the teaching profession, multicultural education, and classroom management.

Linda Fussell

Linda Fussell is a teacher at Brown Barge Middle School, Pensacola, Florida. She is the team leader for the American Tapestry Stream, which was recognized by the National Middle School Association as a First Place Teaching Team in 1996. She is also a member of the Association for Supervision and Curriculum Development, the National Council for Social Studies, and the Organization of American Historians. Her professional interests include multicultural education, authentic assessment, and school reform.

Anne Richardson Gayles-Felton

Anne Richardson Gayles-Felton is a Professor of Secondary Education in the Graduate School at Florida A&M University, Tallahassee. She has served on many local, regional, and national committees, commissions, and boards. She served a three-year term on the Task Force Committee on Teacher Education for the Board of Regents, University System of Florida, a three-year term on the State Board of Independent Colleges and Universities, and a term as a Special Consultant to the Governor's Commission on Quality Education in Florida. She is a member of the State Board Education Advisory Committee on the Education of Blacks in Florida, and also a member of the "Master Teacher" Commission of the Association of Teacher Educators. She has received many awards for professional excellence, including being honored as one of the Seventy Leaders in Teacher Education by the Association of Teacher Educators. She also was invited to present a paper on multicultural education to the 1996 World Assembly of the International Council on Education for Teaching. Gayles-Felton is a prolific writer, authoring 59 articles, six research studies, and two monographs; she also has co-authored three monographs. Her writings and research activities have focused upon quality teaching and learning, and on multiculturalism.

Cathy Gutierrez-Gomez

Cathy Gutierrez-Gomez is a Professor at the University of New Mexico in Albuquerque. She has been an early childhood education consultant specializing in multicultural education, language and literacy development, and parent involvement.

Gutierrez-Gomez is an NAEYC Multicultural Panel member and has served in various capacities with organizations involved in addressing cultural diversity and racism issues, including the Dallas, Texas, chapter of the Anti-Defamation League of B'nai B'rith. Gutierrez-Gomez has 18 years' experience working with early childhood programs, including Head Start and private child care. She is currently serving as a board adviser for Peacemakers, which focuses on helping American Indian youth develop cultural identities and leadership skills.

Phyllis Y. Hammonds

Phyllis Y. Hammonds is an educational consultant who provides training and technical assistance to educational institutions (public/private) and nonprofit organizations across the United States. She has over 20 years of experience working with Head Start programs in the areas of early childhood education, family/parent involvement, cultural diversity, staff development, and family literacy. Hammonds is a doctoral degree student in Curriculum and Instruction, with a specialty in Reading and Language Studies at Southern Illinois University at Carbondale.

Socorro Herrera

Socorro Herrera is an Assistant Professor of Elementary Education in the College of Education at Kansas State University, Manhattan. She is an instructor of ESL Methods, ESL Assessment, and Linguistics. She is also the Director of the ESL Distance Education Program that began in the fall of 1996. Her most recent research and professional development activities, much of them conducted through the Midwest Desegregation Assistance Center, have concentrated on bilingual/ESL strategies and assessment techniques for grade-level educators in districts throughout Kansas, Iowa, and Missouri, especially those districts that serve a significant number of Mexican American students. Her professional interests include: Mexican American studies, bilingual and ESL instruction, multicultural education, the assessment of culturally and linguistically diverse (CLD) K-12 students, and postsecondary CLD student recruitment and retention.

Robert Hilliard

Robert Hilliard is an Associate Professor in Middle Grades and Secondary Education at the State University of West Georgia Carrolton. Hilliard has served as Director of Professional Development Schools at West Georgia and has held the position (in other universities) as Director of Field Experiences and as a public school central office administrator. He has served on the Board of Directors for the Association of Teacher Educators and on the Professional Preparation and Certification Committee for the National Middle School Association. His professional interests include diversity education (multicultural, gender, and inclusion), middle level education, supervision, management, and motivation.

Donna Imatt

A middle school education enthusiast, Donna Imatt has been a Brown Barge Middle School teacher and integrative curriculum writer since 1991. Imatt has written and taught curriculum "streams" titled: "Global Awareness," "Conflict & Compromise," "Historical Motifs," and "Work Hard, Play Hard." In addition, Imatt has taught conflict resolution for the University of West Florida, co-authored curriculum materials with the Escambia County, Florida, Core Values Initiative, and has served as an integrative curriculum consultant for Florida's Department of Education. Her current professional interests include integrative thematic learning, conflict resolution, and continuous learning.

Elaine Jarchow

Elaine Jarchow is Dean of the College of Education at Texas Tech University, Lubbock. She holds degrees from Ohio State University and Kent State University. Her major research area is international education; specifically, curriculum decision-making in emerging democracies, and cultural awareness in international student teaching and faculty exchange settings. She has served as an education consultant in China, Thailand, Egypt, Ghana, New Zealand, Australia, Mexico, Belize, Poland, and Honduras. She is the author of more than 50 manuscripts, over 50 conference presentations, and 18 funded grants. She chairs the American Association of Colleges for Teacher Education's Committee on International Education, and is a member of the Association of Teacher Educators' International Affairs Committee, Global Education Task Force, and Publications Committee. She is the Treasurer of the World Council for Curriculum and Instruction, and a member of the International Council on Education for Teaching's Board of Directors.

Patricia J. Larke

Patricia J. Larke is a Professor in the Department of Educational Curriculum and Instruction at Texas A&M University, College Station. She is developer of the Multicultural Mentorship Project and teaches graduate and undergraduate courses in multicultural education. She previously chaired the Association of Teacher Educator's Professional Journal Committee and is currently serving on NCATE's Review Board. Her professional interests include multicultural education, educating teachers for diverse classrooms, and issues of concern to teachers of color.

P. Rudy Mattai

P. Rudy Mattai is Professor of Educational Foundations and Director, Center for Interdisciplinary Applied Research in Urban Issues at the State University of New York (SUNY), Buffalo. He received a Ph.D. in Foundations of Education and International & Comparative Education from the University of Pittsburgh. He is the recipient of several academic awards and grants, including a FIPSE Comprehensive Program award, NEH Fellowship, and the President's Award for Excellence in Scholarship and Research at SUNY, Buffalo. His major research and publications are in the area of cultural diversity.

D. John McIntyre

D. John McIntyre is Associate Dean for Teacher Education in the College of Education and Professor in the Department of Curriculum & Instruction at Southern Illinois University at Carbondale. McIntyre's research has focused on the areas of teacher education and instructional supervision. He is a Past-President of the Association of Teacher Educators (ATE) and is the Co-Editor of the annual Yearbook Series on Research in Teacher Education.

Kevin Murry

Kevin Murry is an Assistant Professor of Foundations and Adult Education in the College of Education at Kansas State University, Manhattan. He is currently an Instructor of Multicultural Education, ESL Methods, and ESL Linguistics. He also serves as the Coordinator of the new ESL Distance Education Program at the University and a Professional Development Specialist for the Midwest Desegregation Assistance Center. His most recent research and professional development activities have emphasized: 1) the cross-cultural dynamics of professional interactions among grade-level teachers, school administrators, and their culturally and linguistically different students; and 2) the dynamics of critically reflective practice as a foundation for teachers' ongoing professional development, including direct intervention with districts in five regional states. His professional interests include: multicultural education, cross-cultural dynamics, distance education, qualitative research methods, and reflective practice.

Robert L. Perry

Robert L. Perry is Head and Professor of African American Studies at Eastern Michigan University. He served as Chair and Professor of the Department of Ethnic Studies for 27 years at Bowling Green State University, a department that was organized under his leadership. He received a Ph.D. in Sociology from Wayne State University in Detroit, Michigan. His research and teaching specialities are in race and crime, ethnic relations, Black studies, and urban planning.

Walter S. Polka

Walter S. Polka is Superintendent of Schools of the Lewiston-Porter Central School District in Youngstown, New York. He received an Ed.D. from the State University of New York (SUNY) at Buffalo. He is a member of several national and international organizations, including Phi Delta Kappa and the International Society of Educational Planning, and he has served as a consultant to the Hudson Institute. He has authored several professional journal articles, primarily in the areas of curriculum research and improvement and Customized Learning Plans.

Richard R. Powell

Richard R. Powell is an Associate Professor in the Division of Curriculum and Instruction at Texas Tech University. In addition to teaching qualitative research, curriculum theory, and cultural diversity courses, Powell is the Director of the West Texas Environmental Project. His research in the areas of teacher education, culturally sensitive teaching, middle level teaching, and curriculum integration have been published widely. He is co-author of several books, including *Field Experience: Strategies for Exploring Diversity in Schools* and *Classrooms Under the Influence.*

Nancy L. Quisenberry

Nancy L. Quisenberry is Interim Dean of the College of Education and Professor in the Department of Curriculum and Instruction at Southern Illinois University at Carbondale. She has degrees from Indiana State University and Indiana University in the fields of Home Economics and Elementary Education (Early Childhood/Linguistics). Her major

areas of teaching and research are early childhood, language arts/language development, and teacher education. She is the author of two books, numerous journal articles,
chapters in books, and reports. She was a member of the NCATE Board of Examiners for
10 years, a member of the Board of Directors of the American Association for Colleges
of Teacher Education for two terms, was Folio Coordinator for the Elementary Education
NCATE Folios for the Association for Childhood Education International, and is Treasurer of
the U.S. National Committee to the World Organization of Early Childhood Educators
(OMEP), Secretary-Treasurer of the Association for Childhood Education International,
and President-Elect of the International Council on Education for Teaching. She served
as ATE's Chair of the Commission on Racism From a Healing Perspective.

Ronald Rochon

Ronald Rochon is an Associate Professor and Assistant Dean in the College of Education
at the University of Wisconsin - La Crosse. He teaches social foundation and multicultural education courses. His research interests focus on contemporary African American
college students' perceptions and maintenance of their ethnic identities and cultural
heritages.

Halloway C. Sells

Halloway C. Sells has a doctorate in Organizational Management and Development
from the Social Psychology Department, as well as graduate degrees in Community
Planning and Public Administration from the University of Cincinnati, and a Master's
in Social Work from the University of Michigan. Sells served as Executive Director of
a human service agency, The Seven Hills Neighborhood Houses, Inc., while he was
Assistant Professor at the Psychology Institute, University of Cincinnati. He has
served as Associate Director of the Cincinnati United Way. Currently, he serves as
Senior Professor at The Union Institute, College of Arts and Sciences. He has been on
faculty at the Institute's graduate school for 23 years.

G. Pritchy Smith

G. Pritchy Smith is a Professor of Curriculum and Instruction at the University of
North Florida in Jacksonville. He is one of the founders and a past Vice President of
the National Association for Multicultural Education (NAME), and he served on
NAME's Board of Directors (1990-97). He has conducted research on the impact of
admission and certification tests on the racial and ethnic composition of the national
teaching force; he also is author of several articles about multicultural education, as
well as a forthcoming book on knowledge bases for diversity in teacher education.

Gwendolyn Trotter

Gwendolyn Trotter is Professor and Director of Student Teaching at Central Michigan
University, Mt. Pleasant. She was formerly Professor and Coordinator of Curriculum
and Research in the College of Education at Florida A&M University in Tallahassee.
She received her degrees from Southern Illinois University. Trotter was previously a
tenured faculty member at Loyola University of Chicago and was employed for 20
years there. At Loyola University, she was Director of Teacher Education and Special

Assistant to the Dean of the School of Education. She also has served as visiting professor and administrator at Grambling State University. She has been a consultant with many colleges, universities, professional organizations, and associations. She also developed a research collaborative project in 1988 at Grambling State that encourages and aids minorities to join professional organizations. Her "researching teachers-in-residence" model has been implemented at University of Tennessee at Martin, LeMoyne-Owen, and Loyola University of Chicago. This model is currently being implemented at Florida A&M. Trotter's creative activities also include being the lead consultant in the development of a co-project of the National Council for Accreditation of Teacher Education (NCATE) and the American Association of Colleges for Teacher Education (AACTE).

Porter Lee Troutman, Jr.

Porter Lee Troutman, Jr., is an Associate Professor in the Instructional and Curriculum Department in the College of Education at University of Nevada, Las Vegas. He teaches courses in multicultural education and elementary education. Troutman has served as Director of Teacher Corps, Student Teaching, and he has chaired the College of Education's Diversity Committee. He is one of the original founders of NAME (the National Association of Multicultural Education), and he recently established a NAME state chapter in Nevada. Other professional responsibilities include being an evaluator for NCATE and the U.S. Department of Education Blue Ribbon Schools Program. Troutman also received a Fulbright-Hayes Fellowship to study diversity and culture in Singapore. He is a member of the ATE Commission on Racism. His professional interests include multicultural education, MCE professional development, and at challenge children.

Larry A. Vold

Larry A. Vold is an Associate Professor in the Department of Professional Studies in Education at Indiana University of Pennsylvania. He coordinates the Philadelphia Urban Program, which places inner-city students into preservice field experiences, internships with community centers and social service agencies, and student teaching slots. Vold also coordinates an International Student/Faculty Exchange Program with the European Teacher Education Network, a consortium of colleges in Denmark, England, Finland, the Netherlands, Norway, Spain, and Sweden. He has been active in ATE at the national and state levels. His professional interests include the development of field experiences and service learning, the process of socialization into the profession, multicultural education, partnership and community involvement, and policy issues of equity and equality.

Gwendolyn Webb-Johnson

Gwendolyn Webb-Johnson is an Assistant Professor in the Department of Educational Curriculum and Instruction at the University of Texas at Austin. Her research interests include teacher development among preservice and inservice educators, with a focus on multicultural transformation, the recruitment and retention of culturally diverse teachers, culturally relevant classroom management, and special education.